Please
take a moment —

And pass it on
to someone else.

I'll see you on
the bench,

Arte
July 2024

THE
OLD MAN
ON THE BENCH

A Beautiful Day

ANNE DANIELLE GINGRAS

BALBOA.
PRESS
A DIVISION OF HAY HOUSE

Balboa Press books may be ordered through booksellers or by contacting:

Balboa Press
A Division of Hay House
1663 Liberty Drive
Bloomington, IN 47403
www.balboapress.com
1 (877) 407-4847

Because of the dynamic nature of the Internet, any web addresses or
links contained in this book may have changed since publication and
may no longer be valid. The views expressed in this work are solely those
of the author and do not necessarily reflect the views of the publisher,
and the publisher hereby disclaims any responsibility for them.

The author of this book does not dispense medical advice or prescribe the use
of any technique as a form of treatment for physical, emotional, or medical
problems without the advice of a physician, either directly or indirectly. The
intent of the author is only to offer information of a general nature to help
you in your quest for emotional and spiritual well-being. In the event you use
any of the information in this book for yourself, which is your constitutional
right, the author and the publisher assume no responsibility for your actions.

Any people depicted in stock imagery provided by Getty Images are
models, and such images are being used for illustrative purposes only.
Certain stock imagery © Getty Images.

Print information available on the last page.

ISBN: 978-1-9822-2622-0 (sc)
ISBN: 978-1-9822-2623-7 (e)

Balboa Press rev. date: 08/27/2019

It's a beautiful day!

To my father who throughout life taught me to see how we are blessed to be given the privilege of breathing in the daily splendor which surrounds us everywhere we go. As he would always say: "It is indeed a beautiful day!"

Je t'aime Papa
xo

CONTENTS

ABOUT THE OLD MAN

Over the past few months, I've received numerous questions regarding "the Old Man." Is he real? Do I speak to him and listen to his voice? The answer to all these questions is: yes. The Old Man is real, and we have regular discussions. He speaks to me through family members when things become difficult, and I forget how to be grateful for my many blessings. He speaks through me through colleagues and students at work, when I need to be reminded that we are all on different journeys – doing the best we can with what we know – at that very moment. He speaks to me through the words of strangers who become friends through 'coincidental' meetings at supermarkets, or while sitting in airports. He talks to me through my plants. He whispers through my musical compositions. He is present as I walk the path on my daily journeys. He watches over me while I sleep and often sits with me, on an actual bench, by a flowing river. You see, the Old Man is timeless. He has existed before you and I were even specks of energy. He knows all and creates all. As I get older, and hopefully wiser, I sense His presence even more in everything. I trust Him. I talk to Him. I respect Him. He is there, always. This book is a collection of some of our conversations. Many months ago, I decided to listen and shared with you some of the things that He taught me. The lessons continue. Here are some more of our most intimate moments and conversations.

ABOUT BEING MARRIED TO A MYSTIC (WORDS OF MY HUSBAND)

Roughly 91 million miles (it varies) from a small star, three planets into a solar system lies a blue world that is almost 8,000 miles wide, which spins at approximately 1,000 miles per hour, and flies through space at 67,000 miles per hour. It takes this planet nearly 24 hours to complete one spin, and 365 days, more or less. To circle the star which holds it in its orbit. This results in a gravitational pull of 9.78 meters per second (squared). Its proximity to the sun, plus a plethora of other factors too numerous and frankly irrelevant to my point has made it a relative lottery winner amongst other planets in that it sustains life. (This is of course up to some debate as 'winner' is a term I am sure the earth is not always feeling due to the nature of some of its inhabitants).

Moreover, that, my friends, through the magic of the internet and several millennia of these inhabitants evolving and looking inward and outward and poking and prodding and kicking the tires, we now understand how we humans can stand up and not fall off this world at these horrific speeds and thus burn up then freeze and go back to being stardust, rather than walking around wearing cloth coverings, styling the hair (or lack thereof) on top of our craniums and debating whether any of this really matters.

It is a part of the human condition to try to explain things. To measure, to explore, to quantify that which we perceive so that we understand why. To soothe our intellect and thus demonstrate how it is we are so lucky. Through the years, I have taken a minor interest in physics and now mostly understand how these statistics are what has led to me being able to sit here and articulate myself. However, in reality, I don't need to understand any of it to enjoy it. None of us do. We can get up in the morning, brush our teeth and shower, go to the bathroom, don our cloth coverings and make our way through our lives, earning odd pieces of metal and paper (or now just electronic numbers) that buy us sustenance and lodging and Netflix, only to go to sleep and start the insanity all over again the very next day.

We do not need to understand it to enjoy it. We don't need to understand the mechanics of a vehicle to enjoy one. We don't have to know how a particularly fine wine is made, or beer is brewed, or how the internet works, to enjoy them. We appreciate them.

Thirty years ago, I met a gorgeous redhead who captivated me and turned my world on its head and made me somewhat understand that I knew so little. So in the ensuing years, two children (now adults), seven dogs, three houses, numerous cars, and so many other things, I have, like many other people, pursued my intellect in an attempt to understand Anne. To see what makes her tick. All for the good of myself of course and all to make reason of my existence. So it has taken me all these years to grasp that this is just not possible. However, I do not mean this in a misogynistic manner. I live with this beautiful person. I want to know. So I have figured out that I can't figure it out.

Anne is indeed one of a kind. As the years go by, her potential is slowly revealing itself, and it is something to behold. She is so much: a mom, a wife, a friend, an educator, an Aspie, a loner, a brilliant writer, an old heart, a dog lover, a restless soul, a timeless entity, but most of all, a mystic. A mystic by one definition is 'a person who seeks by contemplation and self-surrender to obtain unity with or absorption into the Deity or the absolute, or who believes in the spiritual apprehension of truths that are beyond the intellect.' That definition does not cut it for me. I would say 'deep to the point of infinity' might be closer. Not even Anne understands Anne - yet. She has done her 'shift' as the mom of children. This lady is an educator to be sure, but that pays the bills. If you were to ask her what she does, the educator would likely be far down the list, although as a teacher she is most impressive. Of course, she is. She does well at everything she tries. However, she is SO much more.

Many have asked me the very questions I have often asked myself. What makes her tick? Why does she do the things she does? Why so many projects? Why so busy? I have to tell you all right here, right now.... give up wondering. I have done so for quite a while now, and it helps. There is no quantifying Anne. There is no 'raison d'être.' At least not in any way we puny bipeds can comprehend, and that's okay.

Just do like me. Enjoy it. Prepare to be amazed!

ABOUT LIFE JOURNEYS (CIRCA NOVEMBER 2018)

I just came back from my parents' condo. It's the last weekend that we will ever be in there: it's all but been emptied. Tomorrow, we walk in and clean it up. The walls will be painted next week. The new owners are excited. Years of memories and lifetimes of our stories have been packed up. Some have been shared with others. Some others have been given away while others have simply been discarded. It's funny how time went by so fast. I still feel like a teenager, young, thinking about my future and what I wanted to be and where I was going to live. I never once imagined that my parents would one day grow older and that I would become their primary caretaker. I know. We all go through it - everybody does. I know. However, this is different because it's been our family's journey. I have never been so drained and exhausted. Happy and relieved. Torn inside and broken. You know the drill - maybe. In the past few months, I've cried – a lot. I've screamed. I've laughed. I've mourned. As a human being, it's been tough. As a daughter, it's been often unbearable. Because of this journey, I feel that I've become that much more resilient. I've learned to pace myself and to allow myself to live through the motions and the emotions. It has just made me more aware of how time is precious and how living your dreams and passions is a must. One must carefully plan for the future - but also pluck the flower of today - as my Mother used to say. Live well. Be good to others. Foster no regrets for it wastes precious time and energy - time that should be spent making memories. Accomplishing dreams. Living out dreams from your bucket list. Living. Laughing. Loving.

I need to share with you that I could never have done this alone and that my family has saved me (yet again). My husband and my sons have been the ones who did so much. They are the ones who held me as I cried and sobbed uncontrollably. They've moved tons of stuff (literally). They were my rocks. Along with my son's girlfriend - they walked me along my journey - one that I could have never accomplished without their undying love and support. I will forever be grateful ...

Finally, to my family and friends who messaged us, encouraged us, helped us, sent me love and light: merci. You made the difference. You have saved us and helped us retain our sanity.

What's next? Wine. Lots of it. Probably a few bottles here and there. To celebrate, toast and to move on. I have projects to complete: new chapters to write (literally), music to compose, journeys to explore. I hope that my husband can rest a little bit - he's spent and deserves it. May my boys be able to breathe a little easier, knowing that we have helped complete a most incredible life journey for my parents and ourselves.

Onwards. It's time. The walls spoke to me one last time, but the memories will forever be engraved in my heart and Spirit. In Life, there are times when we need to move on: and that's okay.

Message from the Old Man: *"Today is a good day to collect beautiful moments: cultivate kindness and be brave with your life. Come what may, ALWAYS follow your heart and remember that happiness heals."*

REFLEXIONS ABOUT A PASSING SEASON (SUMMER 2018)

Life is about looking back at memories, smiling (or healing) and then looking at what is, now, at the moment. Do not dwell on what was - or even worse - on what 'could have been' - breathe in the moments of your life and be thankful for the moments you have been given. I'm smiling this morning - the air is cold and crisp: it feels like another chapter is about to begin, as it always does in September when I get ready to go back to work. What an epic Summer this was: I was fortunate to travel, to write, to relax, to find myself in my second and third homes and to bring back picturesque memories. No, the weather did NOT cooperate as we had hoped it would - but some things are out of my hands, so I wore jeans and sweatshirts. I found my cute umbrella and at times chose to hibernate within the confines of my River House. In the end, it all turned out pretty good.

It's Friday and a fresh, untainted weekend awaits. It's time to take the time to BE, to merely sit, have a simple cup of coffee and be still - listen to the sounds of Life around you - and more importantly - listen to the voices in yourself. What are they telling you about yourself? About others? What are perhaps the next steps in your journey - ones that you can take *today*? Don't wait until tomorrow - dreams start somewhere and today could be the first step required to begin realizing one. Whether you're planning to clean out a closet, or publishing a future best-selling novel: a goal is a goal, and little goals lead to big dreams being accomplished.

Carpe Diem - as they say.

Message from the Old Man: *"Seize this day. Smile. Laugh. Live. Love. You may just be surprised at the outcome".*

ON BEING BULLIED
(AN OBLIGATORY REPRINT)

My mother used to tell me this so very often: "People say sticks and stones may break your bones, but names can never hurt you …". Although she meant well, this didn't prove to be true, at least not in my case. I was severely bullied as a child, as a teenager and later on as an adult. I still hurt to this day, but I feel compelled to share some moments with you so that you understand where I am writing from, and how I do appreciate when someone comes to me, feeling belittled, scared and afraid of what happens next. The fear. The sense of being powerless. The shame

It is Pink Day across our school board today: pink here – pink there. What a great message that being bullied is not acceptable – and that taking a stand is essential - AND THE RIGHT THING TO DO. Though I have finally managed to overcome the overall mental anguish, I never will forget how difficult it was/is to ignore it – and to forgive the ones who inflicted it upon me …. Growing up was severe enough: growing up with having Asperger's AND having red hair was even worse. *Ketchup hair. Medusa. Dummy. Freak.* All names that sometimes still resonate at times when things get quiet, and I am left with my thoughts. I hope that these mean girls are doing well these days... and can't help but wonder if perhaps they have experienced the same pain. Maybe they have come to understand what they did and the effect it had on my growing up. I hope that their hearts are at peace and that Life is finally treating them well because to be able to inflict that much pain on another human being, one has to be significantly wounded and broken themselves.

As an adult, I also had to deal with being bullied to the point where I exuded signs of physical distress …. but now, I can see that this time, it was due to jealousy…. and so, I have let it go…. Forgiven (yet not) forgotten – *just let it go….* It doesn't make it easier – it only offers a possible explanation to actions which are deplorable and quite sad. I was strong and overcame it … however, I often think about what may have transpired had I not been the person who refused to go on like this … We see on the news countless young people who choose to end their lives instead of going on with daily torment, and I am so very grateful that deep down within me, I was able to find the light worth pursuing and that I am still here to write about it: things could have been different …

In a perfect world, we should be all equal. Understood. Respected. However, this is not an ideal world. So please, if you see someone who is being bullied, step in. Say something. Help the person out, because to not do so is just as bad as the one inflicting the pain. Trust me – as a person who lived through it —- we thank you for it.

Also, a word to my real friends: then and now: thanks for making me realize that I am a person worthy of good things in life …. One day, I'll repay the favor…

I am worth it … (PS - to the ones who bullied me - you would have liked me … just saying!)

Please honor Pink Day - whenever or wherever you may be today. There are children, teenagers and adults who need you to be there for them because at this moment, they are fighting for their very lives, every day - whether it be mentally, physically or spiritually.

Message from the Old Man: *"When you realize and accept that everyone on your daily journey is intended to make you a kinder, more empathetic human being – you will truly be on your way to understanding that we are all connected as One."*

ON FLYING HIGH: A FINAL HOMAGE TO PAPA ROGER (FEBRUARY 2018)

Today, I have the immense privilege of thanking a man who left us on an early February morning, after a brave fight against a debilitating stroke a few weeks ago. I am talking about my father in law, Roger Gingras, my second dad – *le beau Père* as I affectionately have been calling him for the last 25 years of my adult life. He indeed was one of the original old men in my Life.

Thank you for accepting me into your family with open arms, with love, unconditional love – every day for the past almost 30 years. You and I sat for many hours in silence, just being together, watching tv or watching the peaceful waters of my River House (which you so beautifully built for your own family many years ago ....) You never asked for anything. Never judged anything and you had the most optimistic outlook on Life. I'd share my dreams, and my ideas with you and you would always nod your head and say: oui – bonne idée and you'd cheer me on. I saw you hold my husband as he went through the passages of his own life – at times – tumultuous and uncertain – yet you showed him how to treat people: with optimism and dignity. Positivity and grace. You never complained when you were sick or not in a happy place – you treated everyone as we should all do: believing that they were doing the best they can with what they knew – at that moment.

You were a dreamer. You were a visionary. You were my children's best friend and my rock, and now you are gone.

I don't like sharing you with the Angels in Heaven right now. I'm selfish – as I would have loved to hold your hand just a little longer, to talk to you one last time and to kiss your forehead as you fell asleep but in true Roger form, you chose your time to depart to be with your family and friends when the time was right. Today, I can only hope that as you look down upon your children and your family – that you glow in pride, knowing that you were the patriarch of such a robust, beautiful family. It is a shame that not everyone had the chance to see the heart and the Spirit that was Roger Gingras. Godspeed Papa Roger. You will be forever loved and missed. I love you and will see you in Spirit World.

As a final goodbye to you, I would like to share the words that my Alex penned Monday, in your honor, as one of your grandchildren and best friends: (great fans of Game of Thrones …)

"We say farewell to Roger of House Gingras today. He has defended his realm with strength and honor and has been a strong father to his kin. He has been welcomed to the afterlife by the old gods and the new. We shall never see his like again. Now his watch has ended.

May you be proud and fly high." *Je t'aime. xo*

Message from the Old Man: *"Honour your Heart. Honour your memories. Hold close to your consciousness the anniversaries of special moments of your journey. Be still. Breathe. Send out light and love to those ready to receive it. Love knows no distance and travels all realms of Time and Dimensions".*

ONCE UPON A TIME

Once upon a time, a few fortnights ago, she decided to change her Life forever. At the time, it seemed impossible because she was exhausted in all the aspects of her existence: her body was craving sleep and rest, her mind no longer could think straight, and her Spirit had started dwindling. She felt sad, cold and so lost.

Once upon a time, surrounded by a loving family, she went back to her River House and cried for a few days, erasing from her heart the remaining tears of years which had flowed by so quickly. She forgave those who had hurt her. She let go of things that she could no longer control and accepted what is as well as what was meant to be. She observed the stroke, the autism, the Alzheimer's and the other health woes. She cried for herself, for her family, for her friends. Then, when all her tears had flowed, surrounded by the gentle sounds of her snoring fur friends, she fell asleep and soared away on the clouds. She floated for days, surrounded by the serenity of the peaceful rocking of the Universe. She slept, slept and slept some more until she no longer felt like sleeping.

Once upon a time, while in Dreamland, her Guides told her that it was time to get up. On a cold winter morning, she felt them help her get to her shaky feet. She stood up. She got dressed up and finally was strong and brave enough to show up. On that particular morning, as she looked outside, she knew the time had come to change everything in her Life. Surrounded by the Love of her family, she began the process. She turned on her favorite music, closed the door to her office and started cleaning it out. She threw out papers which no longer served a purpose. She read through old letters. She found old journals which described in great details whom she had once been. She found pieces of herself which had long disappeared, and she smiled. She knew where she had been, where she wanted to go and she now, at this very junction in time, understood where to start.

Once upon a time, she decided to reinvent herself. It seemed as though, and felt like she had fallen from her cloud, but as always, her Angels and Guides picked her up and held her until she was ready to walk alone. She took the printer out of her thinking room. Work would no longer be performed in her sacred personal space. She drew open her drapes and welcomed in the sunshine. The window was open, and the cold winter crisp air filled the room. The desk was moved and now offered a view of her graceful trees. The birds were singing, and once again, she smiled.

Once upon a time, she decided to reinvent herself - Mind. Body. Spirit. She began to eat only foods that would make her strong and healthy. The food she chose to eat would no longer hurt any living being, and it would honor her body. She began to silence the voices of negativity. She surrounded herself with her Family and began to re-explore the depths of her Mind and her Soul.

Once upon a time, she watched *Netflix* and smiled. She traveled to Paris. England. Bali. She studied the cuisine of acclaimed Parisian chefs. She took an imaginary trip to New York and lived vicariously through the eyes of Miss Bradshaw. She toured all over the world with Mr. Grey. She slept. Ate. Read. She slowly rebuilt herself, cell by cell. Moment by moment. Day by day.

Once upon a time, she heard that people were gossiping about her and she smiled. She had fallen hard and would never come back out. *She had burned out* - they said. She lost it. However, this time she felt amused because they had no idea how wrong they were. The truth is that for the very first time in her adult life, she was coming into her own. Like the small caterpillar taking her time, she cocooned herself even further and ignored the whispers of the World for just a while more. Her family surrounded her. She started breathing every so profoundly: the transfiguration had begun.

Once upon a time, she greeted the morning by opening her eyes, and she determined to be brave. For years, she had been plagued by physical pain. It was the season to transform that. Helped by a beautiful like-minded soul, she began rediscovering her body - movement by movement. Gently and ever slowly, she started to feel her breath as she begins to shift. She felt more flexible and more energetic than she had ever been. Once again, she noted the rumors emerging from the shadows. *She had given up*, they stated. No one knew where she was or what she was up to. It was evident that she would not be around for a while. She grinned and for the first time in months, she posted a picture of herself on social media. There were comments - hundreds of them, and the shadow voices became quiet. They didn't know what was happening, but the results were evident: she had found her way, and she was never going back to where she had been.

Once upon a time, she had a reverie. Her Guides had given her their blessings. She began to meet people again - sharing messages of insights. She was stronger than ever. Clear. Precise. It no longer mattered what they said, for she had found herself and become whole again. Messages poured in from individuals. Insights came from Spirit World. Her body was slowly becoming leaner and stronger and she, for the first time, had grown into the person she was meant to be. She knew that her journey was only beginning. People around her had also changed. She had long stopped paying attention to the voices of what had been and now chose to focus on what was: mindful of her actions, of her food and her breathing. She knew that the biggest test of her current journey was upon her and she smiled. She took a deep breath. She was ready.

Once upon a time, she finally awakened. She chose to stand up, she got dressed and finally, at long last, showed up.

Once upon a time, she never looked back. She wasn't going home. She concluded that she had always been there: she had just chosen to let her inner light shine within herself.

(to all those on my current journey thank you for your love and light xo)

Message from the Old Man: *"BE your story. Become that character who fascinates and inspires others to become a better version of themselves. Live. Love. Share your knowledge and wisdom. Transcend your truth and reality"*.

ABOUT LOVING LEROY (OUR FIRST FUR BABY)

Just when I thought I am finally healthy enough to begin writing about Leroy, more tears are involuntarily starting to roll down my cheeks. My eyes sting and have become incredibly swollen and itchy from crying all last night - I have a migraine, and it feels like I am going to be sick... However, those are only physical side effects. The truth is, our hearts shatter from having made a most difficult decision: one of letting one of our beloved fur babies go. We didn't want to do it - but we had to. Letting go is what we needed to do to honor our first ever fur baby after the more than nine years that he's been part of our family. Leroy.

Growing up, I longed for a pet, but it wasn't meant to be. It was only when one of my husband's sisters had her little one, Dusty, that we became smitten with her, and decided to embark on our sentimental journey. Little Leroy – the little tiny shitzu that looked like a small ball of hypoallergenic black and white hair – thus made his debut in our household. On that day, everything changed. He bonded with all of us. He made us laugh. He taught us, through his tremendous spirit, what unconditional love indeed was. Leroy was always waiting for us to pick him up. He fast became my youngest son's play friend and a confidant while he was growing up. Hug. You know the drill: he instantly became part of our family. He went on every family ride. He ate too many treats and was always willing to receive our love and affection. Leroy brought us on the dog-loving journey - and soon came John-John Gingras, another little shitzu (who traumatized him but also became his best friend ...), Moonie, the timid little rescue shitzu who had given up on life, Steve, our little blind dog who briefly touched our hearts, and finally, Bob and Leia, the small mini-schnauzers with the bigger than life personalities. However, it all started with one particular dog who showed us that pets are not simple animals. They have energy: souls who are extraordinary and often more significant than life itself - and that foster the undeniable potential to make our hearts and spirits grow. I now could never live without a furry pet. My house would feel empty but more important: my heart would genuinely feel hollow.

Years went by too quickly, and our little Leroy became ill. He was exhausted; his tiny body carried cancer and had lost most of his vision. On a sad Friday night in June, he let us know that it was time for him to leave our family, and the heart-wrenching decision to see him over the Rainbow Bridge was tearfully made. As I got ready for the final goodbye, I was so grateful for everything that this little one has brought to us. Over the years, he had become my family's best dependable little buddy. Our little 'pepere,' a furry 'old man' figure who went to bed at 8 o'clock every night because he was so tired all the time had chosen his time to leave us, and we would honor him. The tears are still flowing as I think about how we still miss him, and how his presence will never be replaced. My husband always says to never apologize for the love that you give to your animals, for they too are family members. I never did apologize for loving him. I never will. I smile. You can never love too much: EVER. Such is the beauty of our spirit and souls. Leroy validated this for years as he sat amongst our family, and as he watches over us somewhere in Spirit World.

Leroy, now that you're over the Rainbow Bridge eat the treats. Sleep the naps and enjoy the rides. You were one cherished dog. Know that I will always love you and that you've made us better human beings.

I'm sure that Spirit World is that much better with you in it. I'll see you there every night in my dreams. (Dear Old Man, take care of him until, in many years, I make my final journey home to once again be with him ....) xo

ON LOSING A MEMBER OF OUR EXTENDED COMMUNITY

Dear Shannon,

I did not personally know you, but I know 'of' you, and about your tragic end which came to be. Gone too soon, you became a victim of yet another act of senseless domestic violence. Perhaps what hit me most is when I saw the footage of your house last night, surrounded by cars of the local police force. In your windows, I noticed that the Christmas lights were still on .... although yours had forever been dimmed. It's an image which I will never forget. A picture of joy and hope - riddled with incredible rage and sadness ... I hope that wherever you are now, in Spirit World, you are well and finally safe within the arms of those who love you, never to be forgotten by your family, friends, and community you leave behind...

May you be finally happy and free in Spirit World.

Message from the Old Man: *"Do not wait to see if the World needs your help: you need to help the World help and heal itself. Small gestures always matter and help weave the fabric of real unity so desperately needed by all"* ...

BONSOIR PETIT PRINCE

Quand j'étais toute petite, ma mère avait en sa possession un vieux livre qu'elle me prêta, un bon samedi après-midi en juin, alors que le temps était pluvieux et maussade. Je me souviens bien de celui-ci. Il était habillé d'une vieille couverture en papier beige et sentait le fond d'un tiroir. Quand elle me l'avait remis entre les mains, ma mère me dit: ** Fais bien attention car le livre est vieux, mais l'histoire te plaira. Elle te fera rencontrer quelqu'un de spécial qui te demeurera cher toute ta vie. Attention aux personnages car ils sont véritables ... Amuse-toi bien ... **

Ce livre, vous l'avez peut-être deviné, est celui d'Antoine de Saint-Exupéry intitulé Le Petit Prince. Je me revois souvent, dans ma mémoire, relire ce roman des centaines de fois, vivant à chaque fois une différente aventure à travers des yeux du petit garçon aux cheveux blonds. Mon père m'avait même offert du papier et des crayons de couleurs afin que je puisse reproduire les aquarelles de l'auteur. Ce fut un temps magique de ma vie, et je ne l'oubliai jamais.

La vie passa et comme toute chose, on oublie souvent l'importance des moments vécus dans notre jeunesse. Ceux-ci sont souvent tissés d'innocence et nous pensons que leur importance n'est pas primordiale. Cependant, je demeurai toujours fidèle à mon amour et à ma passion pour ce roman. À l'école secondaire, alors que tout le monde ridiculisait lire ces pages ... je les redécouvrais avec mon âme d'adolescente et comprenais de plus en plus pourquoi ma mère m'avait dit que les personnages qui se retrouvent au creux des pages étaient bel et bien véritables. Il me restait cependant à découvrir l'importance qu'aurais ce bouquin si cher dans ma vie personnelle … ce que j'allais faire des années plus tard …

Adulte, je suis devenue enseignante des arts et de la musique. Quelques années dernières, lors d'une remise des diplômes, un homme que j'admire du plus profond de mon être se dirigea au micro pour faire une allocution à ses étudiants. Grand, calme, honnête mais surtout sage, il demeure le superviseur qui à date dans ma carrière, su me toucher au plus profond de mes pensées et de mes convictions personnelles. Ce soir particulier, tenant son discours devant lui, il cita les paroles du roman, prononcées par le renard: «On ne voit bien qu'avec le coeur. L'essentiel est invisible pour les yeux. » Je me souviens avoir souri. Non seulement parce cette personne me rappelait l'essence du Petit Prince en lui ressemblant à travers son apparence physique et son âme incroyable, mais parce que j'avais longtemps oublié l'impact des mots et des idées de ces écrits. En rentrant à la maison ce soir-là, je me commandai une copie du fameux livre, celui de mon enfance étant perdu depuis des années.

L'ai-je relu, vous demandez? Mais bien sûr. Des centaines de fois, en fait. J'étudie la métaphysique. J'étudie la vie. J'étudie mon âme et celle des personnes autour de moi: ce roman décrit si bien toutes ces facettes de notre existence. On oublie souvent comment avoir du plaisir, comment avoir un coeur d'enfant …. Nous négligeons souvent comme communauté ce qui importe dans nos vies : nous sommes menés par le pouvoir, le travail et l'argent … Nos responsabilités d'adulte nous empêchent souvent d'avoir une joie de vivre quasiment gamine, et nous devenons presque victime d'un monde trop sérieux. Quand je relis le Petit Prince, je m'y retrouve – et je me réinvente. Je pense à ma rose – et surtout, à mon propre renard que j'apprivoise à chaque jour, n'est-ce qu'à travers les gestes que je pose envers mon époux, mes enfants, mes amis, mes collègues ou mes élèves. J'aime ce livre. Non – j'ADORE ce livre et j'exulte d'énergie lorsque je le lis et que je découvre des nouvelles choses ou perspectives cachées au sein de ses pages.

En août 2015, je visitais Paris. Je cherchai en vain pour une copie de mon livre chéri. Malheureusement, il ne fut pas de cette partie d'en trouver un que je pourrais ramener chez moi. En attendant, je continuai donc à lire celui qui se retrouvait en ce moment dans les rayons de ma bibliothèque personnelle. Quand j'y retournai en été 2017, il devint premier dans mes choses à rapporter avec moi, dans ma grande valise. (Mission accomplie !)

Tantôt, je me préparerai un bon café et pour quelques instants, je me perdrai au milieu des pages signées Antoine. J'entendrai les paroles du Petit Prince …. Je sourirai en écoutant ses questions et je me forgerai quelques nouvelles résolutions à explorer …

La vie est belle vous savez. Je pense qu'il est temps de la redécouvrir, accompagnée de mon petit ami blond …

(…) « Les yeux sont aveugles. Il faut chercher avec le cœur ». Le Petit Prince

GOODNIGHT LITTLE PRINCE

When I was a little girl, on a cold rainy June afternoon, my Mother lent me one of her ancient books. I remember it well. It was covered in an old brown paper bag and smelled like an old drawer. When she put it in my hands, my Mother warned me to be very careful, because although the book was very old, I would love the story. She added that I would meet someone extraordinary amongst these pages – one who would likely remain special throughout my lifetime. She said to be very careful for the characters were all real.

Perhaps you've guessed that this book is Antoine de Saint-Exupéry's *The Little Prince*. I often see myself in my mind's eye, rereading this novel hundreds of times, experiencing a different adventure each time, pictured through the eyes of a little boy with blonde hair. My Father even offered me some paper and colored pencils so that I could reproduce the original drawings of the author. It was indeed a very magical time in my life.

Life happens, and like every other thing, I forgot the importance of individual moments from my youth. These are often woven with innocence, and we often belittle their importance. However, I always remained faithful to my love and passion for this novel. In high school, while everyone around me laughed as they read the passages, I rediscovered them with my teenage soul and understood more and more why my Mother had told me that the characters were real. I had yet to discover the actual impact that this very book would have in my personal life. I did years later.

As an adult, I became a language arts and music teacher. A few years ago, at graduation, a man whom I admire from the depth of my self walked over to the podium to deliver a message to his graduating students. Tall, calm, honest, he remains the supervisor whom, to date, has touched my career to the core of my thoughts and personal convictions. On this particular night, holding his words before him, he cited the words pronounced by the fox: « We only see with our heart. What is essential is invisible for the eyes. » I remember smiling. Not only was this person reminding me of the little Prince's essence with his looks and incredible soul, but he was doing so by telling me of the impact of the words and ideas I had forgotten. When I came home that night, I ordered a copy of the book, having lost my childhood copy.

Have I reread it, you ask? Of course! Hundreds of times. I study metaphysics. I consider life. I study my soul and that of those around me: this novel describes so precisely all the facets of our existence. We often forget how to have fun – how to have the nature of a child. We often neglect, as a community, what matters in our lives. We are lead my power, work, and money. Our adult responsibilities stop us from having a zest for life, and we often become victims of a world which is way too dangerous.

When I read the Little Prince, I find myself and I reinvent myself. I think of my rose and more importantly, of my fox whom I tame every day, be it through gestures I make towards my spouse, my children, my friends, my colleagues, and my students. I like this book. No – wait – I AODRE this book, and I vibrate with energy when I read and discover new meanings hidden amongst its pages.

In August 2015, I visited Paris. I looked in vain for a copy of my cherished book. I did not, unfortunately, find one that I could take home with me. In the meantime, I will continue to read the one that comfortably sits on the shelves of my library. (In 2017 – when I went back – I found a copy of the novel, and it was the first thing I noticed to bring back home with me in my gigantic suitcase).

Later, I will prepare myself a delicious coffee, and for a few moments, I will lose myself amongst the words penned by Antoine. I will hear the words of the Little Prince and I will forge new ideas and resolutions to explore later.

Life is beautiful you know. I think that it's time to rediscover it, accompanied by my little blonde friend …

(…) "It is only with the heart that one can see rightly; what is essential is invisible to the eye."

The Little Prince

SMALL GESTURES DO MATTER

I just came home. After work, I stopped in at a local café for a few hours and pondered Life. I love sitting there, watching people as I drink coffee and enjoy a cookie (although this one was vegan and sugar-free and quite honestly tasted like cardboard ...) It's okay though because it was all part of today's journey. Today, I lived. I laughed. Moreover, I loved.

Life can quickly become mundane, and one can so easily get lost in the ins and outs of routines. Today was no different for me. Except that I got up a little earlier, moved a bit more and ate no sugar. All pretty good I suppose. However, what matters most are the 'events' which marked this day and made it so special. It started as a day like all others at the center. Kids came in and out. They wrote tests. They asked for some advice. We filled out job applications— fixed some hair. I gave bananas and apples away. I sat with them at lunch. I chatted and laughed. I scolded when I had to, and offered a few words of wisdom to the wonderful teens I have the pleasure of accompanying on their life journey. Kids walked in and out. At lunch, more than thirty of them showed up and enjoyed some time together. (It's the loudest time - but by far my favorite part of the day). Sometimes, it's so crowded that there is no room for any more people. Even the principal has to step over people to get to them - but we don't care. What matters is that they have a place where they are happy, secure, respected and loved.

Perhaps what marked me most today are two moments. At lunch, one of my kids brought me an apple. He said that his parents had bought them at a local farm and that he thought about me - thinking that I would love to taste it. He then told me: "I feel like a hug." He gave me one. Perhaps this was perhaps one of the most marking moments from the pre-teen who doesn't approach many. He also shared with me that being in my center is the best part of his daily routines. I smiled. I cried too. Small victories. Huge markings on my heart. He's slowly finding his way. I love that I'm there along with him .... gradually getting to know him a little better every day. Future Anne sees great things for him. Today, he confided in me that he loves sciences and math and that he's going to be a physiotherapist. I believe him, with all of my might. Most of all, I believe IN him...

A little later on, another student showed up. He's one of my younger kids. He was tired and wasn't feeling well. He had cried and didn't want to do his work. The sounds were too loud. The lights were too bright. Out came the chess game. I had no plan or strategy but to help him out of his rut. It worked. He laughed along with me. He touched my hands. But at the end of the game, he felt well enough to return to class - if only for a few minutes. When he returned at the end of the day - he was drained. I asked him if he needed a hug. He shrugged - which meant yes. So, I hugged him .... and he smiled. It had been such a small gesture yet it yielded such a massive impact on our lives. Today, not only did he gain my undying attention, he captured my colleagues' hearts as well. Sometimes, the teacher shows up and we, teachers, become the students.

The day progressed. I spoke to a few other friends, enjoying their company and loving the fact that they accept me for who I am - Human with my many faults. They don't judge me. They love me for who I am - and for that, I am incredibly grateful. I think that with all the negative energy going around these days, we NEED to get back to these moments and see that the world still offers love and hope and that we are all connected - young and old. As I often tell my colleagues - we are all the same: we happen to be a little older with some different experiences. They teach me as much as I teach them. Moreover, that is the gift.

I'm going to bed tonight smiling. My day was incredible. I lived. I laughed. I loved. So much. I hope that I never forget that moment! Xo

---

Message from the Old Man: *"Begin EXPECTING and ACCEPTING happiness in your daily life."*

ABOUT THE BUNKIE

There is a place at my River House that is sacred to me. A few years ago, when we moved in, it held a hot tub and was a wasted storage room. It has since transformed itself into what holds my precious nights when I need to escape reality. Initially, it had been designed to host guests, my family and some friends (which it did). Over time, it became my yoga space where I would meet early in the morning to stretch out and regain my ability to move ... However, finally, it found its ultimate purpose: to become MY space (yes, yet another one) where I go to think, have a nap or sleep the night away. I lovingly refer to it as my bunkie ... (although the spelling is likely wrong) Also, it saves me and helps me escape to other dimensions. You see, I'm a massive believer in Dreams and the adventures they hold ... and so I think that it's fitting to be able to escape, once in a while, to a magical space where Dreams become a reality.

Initially, the bunkie was decorated in a 'cottage style.' Of course, everything matched but over the months, it started morphing, living a life of its own. It became adorned with my favorite things: all blue, of course. I have the cedar chest from my parents holding treasures — a pine armoire with my favorite pillows. A giant ottoman to sit on and look at the River during the day. The bed is topped with a mattress so comfortable that one never wants to get up again. There is the old typewriter which most probably wrote love letters to many when it was owned by someone almost 75 years ago. Paris is on the walls, in the sheets, and the air. It faces the River and feels like I am miles away from civilization when I enter its space. Visitors will tell you that the energy in there is unique and special. It has a mystical feeling almost and the ones who have had to sleep or visit there say that they are forever transformed. You see, it has magical properties (which, as you know, I believe in). It can hold my space and lead me to transform it into something incredible. The bunkie is almost like an airport to Dreamland - there I choose destinations and leave (I often smile as I see the stars and the moon right before I depart). It's warm. Cozy. Safe and did I mention? Magical.

Last night, after almost three months, it called my name, and I chose to listen. At around 11h00 pm, I walked through the doors and made it back home. The walls became alive. The scents were reanimated, and I could hear my slumber guides welcoming me back. It didn't take long for me to escape to Dreamland. As I looked outside one last time (it was beautiful - light snow was falling, and there was a small glow), I believe that I heard Orpheus telling me that he would hold my hand and my heart as I fell asleep. For the first time in months, I fell asleep instantly - without tossing - without turning - just being held by the magical energy of my healing bunkie. I made it to Dreamland and woke up just a few moments ago.

I am sharing this so that you too can find a spot that is yours - so that you can transform it into your space - your vessel to bring you to your adventures. Life is short and requires you to be present at the moment. However, nighttime is always the enchanted quiet time where you can escape it and explore other universes when you meet other friends and learn different things. Take a moment to reinvent a guest bedroom perhaps and make it into your own space, your own 'bunkie' if you will - and find yourself being transported on the clouds of the Universe.

Life. Is. Good. It's time for another cup of coffee and for pondering life just a little longer.

Message from the Old Man: *"Be Still and Breathe. The answer to your questions often appears in Silence"* ...

DEAR ANTONIA

Every year, on December 8th, I celebrate my grandmother Antonia's birthday.

She passed on to Spirit World when I was only four – and has been my guardian angel all of my Life. She has been there in good times and horrible ones – holding our family together – soothing my aching heart and soul. Many times, I have felt her arms around me – I have sensed her presence in my environment…. I inherited many of my sensing abilities from her. She read tea leaves and made 'stories' from plain playing cards. She often leaves messages out for me – and inspires me through my writings and my music. In my life, I very often feel so alone. I often wonder if I can get through to the next moment …. she is there …. and things are always better because of her presence. She is the third A of my A-Team…

She is a great soul: Talented. Patient. Fair. She is determined to help me become a better and stronger person. She has her work cut out for her: I am stubborn and do not always listen to what she tells me. However, I'm getting there … I am slowly honing my reading talents which I got from her — hoping to make a difference - one day at a time - one heart at a time.

Tonight, I will have a cup of warm water with lemon – in her honor. She loves that — simple pleasures. So later, in Dreamland, we'll meet up again and have another one of our nice long chats. Perhaps laugh at Life – and make plans for what will come next, because I'm sure of one thing: the best is yet to come ...

See you soon Memère. Have a great birthday. Xo

ABOUT DAY TWENTY-SEVEN

It's officially day 27 of my self-reinvention. If you're within my close intimate circle of people, you know that although it looks easy, the work has been continuous, exhausting but incredibly beneficial to my overall self. You see, I am finally taking the time to listen and observe myself, from all perspectives. A personal *CSI*, if you will. I am usually the one who notices when people are about to crash, when they feel sad or when they need to be picked up and rebuilt from within. How different it is when you step out of yourself and realize, with the help of others, that this time it is you who is about to become herself broken unless she stops the bus and jumps off for a while, which I did. How lucky I was, to be honest with myself and with the close people that I needed to rest, for I was exhausted. Life. Circumstances. Events. Happiness and self -disappointment - intertwined within my body - my mind and my soul. I knew I needed the rest when I thought about the things I used to love doing - and I no longer felt like entertaining them. It was like the blinds around me were starting to close - and I just wanted - no - just NEEDED to sleep. So, I did. I chose to self-hibernate.

I napped for months. Although I was awake for many parts of the day - I was merely functioning on automation. I walked the walk - talked the talk - but only for form. For appearances really. I fooled myself, and I fooled others into believing I was whole. It worked - until my inner heart - that little voice that you try to silence with music and distractions - my Intuition - told me: enough is enough. I woke up one day, and I knew that everything had to change. There are pivotal moments in your existence that can be pegged with a particular date. Your engagement. Your wedding day. The birth of your children. I add to this list the date of December 14th, 2016. It's the day that everything changed for me. As I sat with my husband and my trustworthy friend, I admitted that I had become tired. I was exhausted by everything and by everyone. My skin was pale. My energy was gone. My eyes were closed. I knew I needed to have something change when my Guides told me that they were shutting my intuition down for a while. I was no longer going to be able to listen for others - until I heard FOR myself - ABOUT myself. So, it began.

I came home on December 14th, and I cried. I cried all day and all night. When I woke up the next day - I felt better. I had let all the built-up tears which have welled within myself finally pour out. I had cried for my family. My parents. My brother. My children. My husband. My friends. My students. I cried for the World.

Bur most importantly, I had cried for myself - about myself. Then I cried for no reason - but just for the sake of crying. Millions of tears. Puffy eyes and all. When I stopped, I had a massive migraine and puffy eyes. I never looked back. Waking up the next morning, I was still tired - but I had a plan. A real one - and it was going to work. The advice I had been dishing out for years to others that had succeeded was about to be transposed to myself. I knew it would work - it. I decided that I just needed to do it. I no longer wanted to feel like I had been - a radical change in all aspects of my Life was required to get better.

I'll skip the many boring details (they'll be in a book someday), but I can tell you that I am reinventing all aspects of my Life: Body - Mind - Spirit. It takes work. Daily work and it is exhausting. However, as I see results - it also fuels me to keep moving forwards: and I am well on my way. I feel that I am sufficiently advanced to share some of my daily routines - should you find yourself in the same situation as I was a few weeks ago. After years of built up - I was ready to restart. Reboot - and reinvent me.

BODY: I have changed all of my eating habits. I'm seeing a naturopath and consulting with my physician and seeing my healer. Because of allergies and health reasons, I am now trying to follow a plant-based diet. It's worked wonders. Miracles. I'm doing it for energy. For the vitamins and minerals - and because I was tired of feeling like crap. I get looks. Comments. Some encouraging and some disguised as snickers. However, you know, I also get results. I have never felt (or looked) better ... I thank my family for standing by my side on this daily culinary journey. I have moments that hurt. That is difficult and painful. However, they encourage me to keep going - and so I do. I'm starting to glow from the inside out. That is the ultimate prize. Oh - and I put my scale away for a few weeks - for weight loss is NOT the purpose of this shift. That has become THE challenge. We are so conditioned by numbers and society to be like this or weigh like that. Enough. I'm sticking to it. I'm walking. Literally and figuratively.

I've also rested. I take naps. A lot of them. For the years that I did not sleep. For the nights that I worried and tossed and turned. For healing my body and my pains: I sleep now. I go to bed earlier and sleep. If I need a break, I take one. I will no longer neglect my body: I take breaks when I need them and when they are due. I am only as strong as I let myself become - I intend on becoming that much stronger - and powerful.

MIND: You know - the brain is a funny thing. Thoughts grow with what you feed them. Ideas have power - and also Life. Feed them negativity: you get anxiety. Pain. Panic. Worry. So, I've switched it up. I no longer feed my mind darkness, and I change my patterns if I see myself getting there again. I try to live in the HERE. In the NOW. I read books by people who inspire and think about the one I'll write to add to people's collection. I listen to uplifting music and videos. I choose mantras and live by then. I refuse to stick to negative connotations or ideologies. It's a choice. MY choice - and I'm living every one with the personal responsibility attached to each one that I am making. I choose to be like this - or like that. I bought a planner. (a beautiful find for 5 dollars at the flea market). I'm spending time with it every day. I plan my day.

I write my thoughts and am witness to my evolution. I decorate with stickers. Insert quotes. It's becoming an extension of the person that I am and where I am going. It's exhilarating. I've set goals and attached dates to them. Fun and creative things I've always dreamt of doing. I'm walking there - to every one of those moments. Watch me. Because I have a smile as I'm getting there.

I started a writing course. It's for three weeks, but I know that it'll morph my writing style and change my thinking patterns. It already has, as I joined the group of individuals partaking on this journey as I am. It's been a dream of mine to write for years. I'm penning a novel - writing notes and blogs - but I know that this is the defining moment of my journey. I'm doing this and never looking back. You'll find me on the best seller list one day. Perhaps only on mine - but it doesn't matter. I'll take it - whatever it means. If I write for one person and it makes her smile: my job will be completed, and it will have mattered. However, I have big dreams. Big expectations and I intend to live up to them. Also, about music? Stop listening to the same soundtrack of your life. Reflections are found in many places - including what you choose to look to in the car and your home. I have music with a beat that makes me want to dance (and I secretly do so within the confines of my River House). I love it.

SPIRIT: I realized that my Spirit had dwindled. Do you know what your garden looks like in late Fall when everything has turned yet there is that one little leaf refusing to let go? That feeling. A few months ago, I stopped smiling. Wait - let me rephrase this: I stopped 'feeling' the smiles, and I saw it in my eyes. They were blue, and that's it. Now - they glow. Their twinkle is back. I went deep inside myself and spent time with ME. Re-met ME. Spoke to ME and found out what I want to do that makes me smile. I have started a video podcast. I am writing. I am journaling. For the first time in months, the Intuition is back. I can hear again - better than ever. I can dream again. (and that's where I will leave this aspect of my transformation - for this is not the forum required to share this information - I have other avenues for that).

So, you see, it's a journey: a life-changing one. It's long and arduous and requires extreme discipline and energy, but you know what? I am the happiest that I have been in years. I am slowly seeing myself becoming the person I have always envisioned. A moment at a time. Here. Now. I'll see you in Spring - when I awaken with the Earth with the gentle southern breezes around me. Right now, I am resting and gathering my strength to grow stronger every day: Body - Mind - Spirit.

May you find your way on your journeys - and if you need help - I'm here for you. Because I am here - doing THAT. Do it. It's worth every second of the energy you'll invest.

Addendum – I have since then had to restart the whole process. I'm smiling. I'll eventually get it right ...

Message from the Old Man: *"At times, as you struggle to help others, take a step back and explore your journey. Often, it is within yourself that inspiration resides, for the heart of the dilemma breathes within your spiritual obstacles. Start there: within yourself. Act. Realize what makes your heart and spirit soar. The rest will fall into place."*

ABOUT LIFE CHANGES

I blog - and that is part of who I am. I've been doing this for a few years now, and usually, very early on Sunday morning, I find myself sitting in front of my computer while everyone else in the house still sleeps and I reflect upon the past events and ponder about my week. Today is no different, yet it feels entirely alien to me: as I get ready to go back to work tomorrow, I feel anxiety for many reasons, and I realize how the past few weeks have changed me, perhaps forever. I know that I am in 'transition,' that things are changing quickly around me and that my only way to cope is to breathe and attack every moment with calm and hope.

Let's examine this in greater context.

For a few months now, we knew that my youngest son was facing brain surgery. A very eminent possibility, at any time, that he would be brought in and that a dire procedure would be done. Life has a funny way of us thinking that certain events are months away: you turn around and the time has arrived - and there is little you can do except to 'go with the flow.' For days before the event, I did not function - even though my social and professional obligations warranted me to do so. I went to work in a robot-like manner, taught students as best as I could, marked, prepped for the next day, did laundry, visited our ailing parents, did more laundry, ate, played the 'adult', came home, cried for hours, went to bed, could not sleep and repeated the cycle. I have never felt so vulnerable in my entire life. I felt like people were trying to help me, yet I was drowning in my worry. Living life on the autism spectrum does that to you, at times. Your mind plays tricks on you. You 'look' fine but inside you are falling apart - and I was in danger of quickly falling apart. I didn't. I work for a wonderful employer who permitted me to take time to be with my son to assist him before, during and post-surgery. I wanted to take his place - but such was not my journey - I was meant to 'hold' his space and see him through his fears and anxiety, to comfort him while he suffered and to make him smile when his energy had raised enough to permit him to do so. I realized many things during that journey with him. I thanked the Universe for allowing me to be with him - physically and spiritually. He allowed me to be with him - and the 'World' conspired to make it so.

We are still waiting to see what the outcome will be. I'm hopeful. Nervous. Full of anxiety as I don't know what's coming next: I sense that things are ok - but it plays out in the weirdest of ways - making me lash out at people, cry at odd times and shut down around those with whom I should be present. It's not easy, and I am so thankful to be on this path of waiting with my close family and friends - as well as being able to share these moments with others around me. It's hard to accept help - and it's even more difficult to face our mortality - and yet - perhaps as her most significant project for me - the Universe has forced me to confront my own through the eyes of others in my inner circles.

I go back to work tomorrow a changed person. You cannot go through events such as these unmarked, untouched and the same as you were before they transpired. The truth of the matter is that I am not ready yet - and still, I know that I will have to be. There are high expectations. I have not opened any school-related document in weeks for I have not had the energy to do so. There are papers to be marked, lessons to be learned and prepared: LIFE needs to move on and it will. I know that this week will be so extraordinarily demanding and busy, but as always, I will get it done authentically. I will live, laugh with and love the people with whom I interact in my professional way in a very 'real' kind of way. There is no more time to be 'fake.' Life is NOT about being 'fake' anymore: it's about being here, at this moment, and honoring this moment as the important one. As we face more upcoming transitions within our close family circles, I realize that I cannot be there for everyone at the same time and that sometimes, I have to make choices as to which individual I can share my heart spaces, at that moment. I need to realize that if I am exhausted, tired and unable to face things - I need to verbalize it in such a way that I will receive the energy required to keep ME strong so that I can help others do the same. I need to realize that the word NO is a complete sentence and that in the end, who matters are my family and my close friends, never forgetting myself in this ever-evolving picture. I am blessed to have created beautiful spaces within my physical home and through my online presence to permit me to escape when times become tough to navigate. I am strong but I am also human, and I too must, at times, rest my heart and my soul.

I read a meme the other day which stated that if I passed away, they would replace me at work within a week. That hit - and hard. The truth of the words. The harshness of the reality – and the simple fact that we think that everyone – including ourselves - is invincible *yet we are not*. Facing my son's health story, being witness to our aging and ailing parents have taught me in the past few weeks that the ONLY stories which matter, in the end, are the ones about our loved ones. It's about finding the grace to be there for them, and allowing myself to be present for them genuinely, should they need me to be. So for that, I needed to change myself, and I think that I have. I hope that I am becoming a stronger, more compassionate human being by allowing myself to feel the different changes tied to my Life experiences. I hope that I learn to stand my ground in a real gentle way, never forgetting the outcomes of my actions and my words - yet finally honoring myself as a person who needs and deserves to live with peace of mind. Decisions are made. May I have the strength to stand by the ones I have taken and those that will transpire in the next few months. May the Universe continue to shine her light on me and may I never forget how blessed I am to be here, allowed to 'live' these moments with the people whom I love very much.

Welcome Life. I am ready to walk my days with you.

Message from the Old Man: *"Remember that Life is a choice and you choose how to assume it. There are times when the pain will be too incredible to bare: close your eyes and imagine light touching every part of your body. Breathe and feel the gentle warmth enter your heart. Realize that your Guides and your anchor hold your Spirit together on days when you feel that you cannot do so alone. It's okay to fall apart — I am always next to you".*

ABOUT CONNECTIONS

I'm going to put something out there ... something perhaps not new to you. However, to some, it may be interesting. At least, it may be worth considering, if only for a few mere seconds.

It's bustling in my intuitive mind since last night. It has been for a few hours now. I'm not sure what is going on - but I'm even feeling the physical reactions of the messages which they are sharing with me. (No worries - I am fine - I assure you!) My full A-Team is here along with me. However, Nathaniel (one of my higher Guides), is the one suggesting that I write this 'reminder' ... who am I to dispute what he tells me to share?

These days, the 'veil' is thinner and that we are often subject to 'feeling' more, and sensing more if you will. It's not an illusion. It is real. Why not take advantage of these moments ...? to connect with those you love and miss at this very time of your Earth Journey.

It has been proven in a mathematical way (for all cynics out there), that it is possible to move the smallest atoms of the Universe, from where we are. A thought. A second. A whole Universe crossed and reached. As a woman immersed in metaphysical matters, I implore you to consider how wonderful and powerful this is: if you need to 'connect' with somebody, here on Earth or in Spirit World - you can do so. They'll respond - you need to be 'open' to the answers which you receive. So, if you miss someone at the other end of the country, you can reach out to them. If you miss your family member who has crossed over - you still can. Remember that it's not what you 'see' to be around you that always is - it's about 'seeing' with the right mindset - with the right set of 'eyes'... So, go ahead. Open your heart and your mind. Have that conversation. Have a nap and spend a few hours with those you miss and with whom you yearn to be. Your answers may come in the form of a feeling.

A familiar smell. A light touch on your shoulder or in your hair. You may notice patterns of numbers or letters appearing out of nowhere. Things are perhaps displaced around you - or you may smile as you send out your thoughts and energy. There is telepathy between hearts, you know. You can't break invisible ties. These connections are substantial - for they are made at the soul level. To me – that remains incredible and very comforting to know.

Si MON cœur aime TON cœur et que TON cœur aime MON cœur - alors nos DEUX cœurs ne font qu'UN ... (seul coeur) ....

Whomever. Wherever. Whenever. It's up to you - so it's all real.

I find that extremely exciting... I believe .... do you?

Message from the Old Man: *"It's high time to trust your inner voice. The intuitive voice within you should be what brings you forth on your daily journey. Ego and logic create barriers – you will not be able to process all of which surrounds you until you take time to quiet the voice of reason and until you trust even what remains unseen or unfelt by others. Some things can and should only be felt through your own heart".*

ON LEARNING SOMETHING NEW

We all have things that we should think about every day. Last week, I was inspired to announce a weekly feature which will appear on the Postcards from the Soul social media page. I'm not too sure how it's going to work, but I trust my intuitive team - full-heartedly - and so I am trusting that this will make many of us think, evaluate and perhaps find solace in our daily occurrences. (check it out – it's worth the glance).

Yesterday, I went shopping with my guys. It was a busy Saturday in the city, and it seemed that all those around me were looking and acting aggravated (including myself). I found myself speaking louder, losing patience for things which were utterly trivial and I just wanted to throw a tantrum right there, in public, because the energies were so off ... (I don't do well in public spaces, and at times, I feel like I am attacked from strange vibes when I neglect to 'protect' myself before venturing out ....). After we completed 'the trek,' I headed over to my 'safe' place – the book store - and there I wandered through the aisles, looking at things, breathing in sights and sounds of my 'happy place,' waiting for 'inspiration' to hit me. So as I knew it would - it did. There on a table were a few books, calling out my name. Amongst them were a book of poetry and the 'Complete Course in Miracles.'

I also chose another one and made my way to the checkout counter, smiling. Now, these choices may be surprising to you: after all, why would I choose them - at this time - and tell you about it? The truth is, I think that they chose ME ... and as I peered through the pages this morning after sleeping for hours, I found messages peering through the words - ones directed for me and others in my circles. As in anything and everything that I read, I take some advice, leave some information, agree or disagree with some perspectives and ponder many things. I think that the essence is precisely this one: to find ourselves well-grounded in OUR attitudes, we must first observe and study that of others. To not do so is to be polarized in our thinking - and that obstructs our way of seeing and sensing the World around us.

The Universe of the Intuitive Reader is varied and complicated. At times, I need to focus on objective facts. In other matters, I must be tuned in to the frequencies of those in Spirit World. I must be familiar with traditions and customs which are, at times, not mine; therefore, I do not understand them. I need to come from a place of non-judgment and open-heartedness. (it's not always easy - and I study to become better at what I offer you). Researching and reading permit me to do so. In that past few years, I honed my energy skills by becoming a Reiki Master. I researched and wrote about Past lives while obtaining my Doctoral Diploma in Metaphysical Studies and now, I am on my way to becoming a Holding Space Facilitator (google that) ... all in the hopes of obtaining more knowledge, more insights, more information, and more ideas to help others fully realize their full potential. However, it takes work and time - and I think that this is the message of our very first 'Spaces' blog. Take time to learn something new. Read a few sentences a day from an author who is foreign to you - and who perhaps even challenges your current way of thinking. You cannot grow your mind space and your heart space if you feed them only the ideas which you know and understand. You need to get out of the comfort zone and explore what it is that makes the World around you 'tick' ... and finally - you need to figure out 'how' and 'where' you fit in these new ideas and thoughts, at this time, at this moment.

Moreover, so, if you wish to embark on more 'journeys' of your own - be it in person or Spirit - that is our recommendation to you this week: Pick up a new book. Read a few pages and start challenging your mindset. You'll be amazed at the journeys and new paths that you discover.

"The more that you read, the more things you will know. The more that you learn, the more places you'll go." — Dr. Seuss

ABOUT THE HUMAN RACE

I woke up early. The truth is, I didn't have to wake up too much - because I was on the verge of sleep - if there is such a thing. My mind worked overtime and what complicated matters, as a sensitive person, is that I was somewhat able to capture a lot of images and sentiment linked to specific events which marked our lives this past week.

We had the incredible privilege of listening to Eva Olsson. At 94, this spunky and out-spoken woman is one of our last remaining survivors of the Holocaust. She came to our communities, sharing her experiences about what she had faced, but while she had every right to be angry, to be bitter and to 'hate' - the message that she offered was entirely different. She spoke of bullies and acceptance. She voiced that it was ok to be different - *but that it was NEVER okay to be indifferent in the face of adversity.* As the slides rolled on and you could witness in her eyes how she traveled into her heart and memories, she repeated how important it is to realize that we are not living in a world with differences - but that *we have ONE race: the human race.* "Perhaps," she said, "if we give ourselves a chance to learn from each other, we will never experience something as horrible as these events. NEVER use the word HATE she emphasized. Never go to bed angry because things change in a moment."

Fast forward a few hours, where somewhere in Saskatchewan, a bus full of teenagers was traveling to get to a hockey game. An accident happened. In a straightforward instant, multiple lives were lost. Fifteen individuals found their wings and the others were injured. In a swift candid moment - complete lives were destroyed. Moments like these affect individuals, their families, and friends. A whole country mourns with, and for people, we have never met. Such events mark strangers: we are, after all, Canadians and we hold each other in times of happiness and of incredible sorrow.

As I read the news and watched the footage, I sobbed. I still am as I write this short note. I teach kids that very same age. They share some of the very same dreams, have been playing hockey with the very same teammates for years. They are the kids who waste time in class and don't want to read that French novel or write that essay. They are the kids who jump around and make others laugh. However, they're also students with an incredible heart and soul. They are MY students: someone's child, someone's grandchild, someone's friend. We're all connected somehow - because we share so much in a day, whether directly or in a passage. Tomorrow, I'll remember to have just a little more patience. In the long run - the sentences that they will read or write won't matter - what will be the connections that I will have cultivated through our exchanges about such devastating moments - and how to stay resilient and help those who need our support - even if we don't personally know them.

We live in a very poetic world. At times, there is great sadness, and we lose ourselves in moments that do not matter. I'm no different. We pick fights which should have never come about, we emphasize details that do not matter - and then we move on - as if nothing matters - but the truth is - *it does*. Every little intention that we put out there is *essential*. As Eva said: "to change one person is to improve the World. To send our thoughts and light to families we have never met, in our community or throughout the World, can change the World. Words and ideas have power." As I look outside, I see the Moon is heading off to her corner as the sun begins to rise at the other edge of the sky. Poetry in Nature, reminding us that after darkness, light always shines. On cloudy days, remember that the sun is behind the clouds and somewhere sending out its warmth and hope of a better day.

This morning, love a little more. Love those whom you know - and send love to those you haven't yet met or forgiven. If you love someone - tell them. *Show them.* Stop focusing on things that do not matter. Let things go. Move on if you must but don't give hate the chance to live within yourself. Get angry but let things go. Life is short but if you live every moment with intention and with light in mind - you'll have a great one.

One race: the human race. Let's be a united one in our families, in our communities, and our country. Please send thoughts to those who need them. Send Hope to those who have lost it. Send Love to the lonely and broken ones.

Please pass it on.

Message from the Old Man: *"In a world plagued with fear and negativity, we find ourselves seeking answers in the most unlikely places. Many of us travel the World in the hopes of finding refuge and of perhaps shifting our thought patterns which, of course, is a useful tactic in the short run. However, to truly change ourselves, we must go within our heart and Spirit – in what is our true essence".*

ABOUT BECOMING MY TRUE SELF

I sit in front of my screen, not knowing what will be coming out in the next few sentences, yet compelled to share words with you and so, as I usually do, I sit back and wait to see what will transpire. I guess this time, it's once again about Life and about our priorities, how sometimes they take over and we forget to take care of ourselves. Life is short, way too fast and if we're not careful, it will swallow us whole with the fading dreams of what could have been mixed in with the what if I had done that's ...

I have always been a dreamer, and perhaps that is what has managed to save me in this lifetime. There have been so many 'bizarre' adventures: one episode after another - this happening right after that: fights for justice for this, advocacy for services for that. Perhaps the greatest gift has been to realize how resilient and knowledgeable I've become, how I've become versed in the fine arts of debating and organization. I've become an expert on how to exist and have perhaps, in the process, forgotten how to Live - fully live - while enjoying a balanced lifestyle. It hit me last night, as I was soaking in a bathtub at 7 pm. I was exhausted from the emotional impact of emptying my parents' possessions for the past nine months, from the social exhaustion of 'being' someone whom I am not really because I have autism. I have to look like I 'fit' in. I am physically drained because of the food allergy situations which I am currently battling and attacking - and because of a time change which refuses to let go of its relentless grip on me. A few days ago, as the lawyer took the keys to my parents' condo, I glanced over at my husband. He too has never been so drained and tired. It hit me how we had never stopped for years. I felt his exhaustion - his struggles, and how he too was running all the time, without time to 'DO' anything.

Moreover, there I was, at 7 p.m., ready for bed. I had not yet had time to think about others in my family, let alone about myself - and that's when it hit. Something has to change - and mindset and intentions will be the key.

I know that we all have our situations and I'm not, by any means, complaining. I am merely voicing the opinion, MY opinion, that there has to be something that done. Somewhere in our days, there HAS to be time to sit - not worry about what others think or said, what is coming next in the week in terms of others' needs and lesson plans. There should be a time when we can work on our passions, our hobbies, and our future selves. So, I did it. I went to bed last night, so early. I watched a few minutes of a sitcom and fell asleep. Dreamland did not disappoint: it showed me various options. What I could do - what I should do ... All roads led to the same place: the end of this lifetime - yet all were different in their feelings and purpose. It reminded me of what matters: my immediate family (husband, kids), but it also cemented in BOLD CAPITAL LETTERS how I need to even think of what I want to do - what makes me smile and vibrate. In seven years, I will be retiring and moving on to a new adventure - but you know, time is of the essence. Why wait until then to live out my dreams and passions. Life is, after all, what you make it be, non? It is time for me to morph my days and nights, to live a more balanced Mind Body Spirit connection.

I woke up at 4:44 am. I smiled because it was the sign that I had been so desperately craving. I have a plan, and it's time to put it into action. It's simple. Easy and it will work. The truth is, when I leave my career in less than a decade, although I will have made a dent in many hearts, I too will be forgotten and replaced by an eager 20 something-year-old.

It won't matter that I spent hours wondering about this, worrying about that: what will remain is myself - and how I CHOSE to handle the situations. So, today is another day. As I close one chapter, I am starting to open another, but this time, I'm adding in sentences about me and to what I like and need to be doing. There needs to be time to rest - to find ourselves when we feel that we have lost our way - and time to BE. So, that is how the next few months will play out, a moment at a time. For others, but also for myself - for I too matter. I too should care about my Spirit. Do the same - you'll thank yourself for it later.

Onwards .... xo

ABOUT HEARING THE VOICE OF THE OLD MAN IN MY CLASSROOM

I don't often write notes on a Friday night. I am after all a teacher - an exhausted lady after trying to inspire students on their journeys all day. Usually, I would plop down on the bed and let sleep take me over, but tonight I cannot, for today, I was shaken right down to the roots of my heart and soul by none other than an unassuming typical grade nine student.

Let me put you in context. This student is Cameron - your stereotypical little grade, nine adolescent. He talks a lot. Too much. He laughs. Runs around the classroom (I'm not kidding). He bounces up and down and plays hockey for a Triple-A team in the region. What often people don't see in him is the size of his soul. Through his piercing grey-green eyes, he watches others as he interacts with them. He talks to everybody. Makes everybody feel good and doesn't discriminate - he talks to everybody and anybody who will listen to him - all day. Every day. Hiding underneath the tall and still immature teenager who often gets sent to the office for not doing his work or for being late because he was running in the hallways between classes - is a person with an incredible message and today, he showed up.

For the past few weeks in my History class, we've been discussing the residential schools. What happened how it happened. We read about it, did research and watched videos. Cameron heard me talking about that one day, and he told me: you know - my grandmother went there and survived - and then he dropped it. A little later on that week, he said to me about how they were going to celebrate his grandmother's birthday: she passed on December 28th, and they were going to be remembering her by having her favorite meal and a cake with her face on it. Again, he choked up and told me that she had been to the residential schools and survived - and left it at that. (I teach Cameron for almost 3 hours a day. He sits in my classroom first thing in the morning in French class, and then in the afternoon, he's back for my Grade 9 Religion class. Every day, as he sits close to my desk - on the black bench - he grabs the Tic Tacs which I always leave out for him and the other kids, we discuss many things. A few weeks ago, I held his space as he talked about the Saskatchewan hockey players who had lost their lives. Often, we laugh at YouTube videos which he's watched. He marvels at how he can now get the singing bowl to resonate throughout the classroom. Many hours were spent together during this first half of the semester, and as I got to know him better, he started sharing the things that he knew about that hidden part of our history. His family lives in Kipawa - and as he said: I know all about that stuff ... That's when I decided to ask him: would you come and talk to my history class? He looked at me with his big grey-green eyes, smiled and said: "Sure, I can." Then I told him: "You can do it in English - because the conversations that you had about it were in English in your family - I want you to share these memories in a way that makes YOU comfortable." He smiled and said that on Friday, he'd do it. For gum, of course. I laughed and simply responded: "Agreed."

That morning, Cameron showed up late to my classroom: I was hungry he said - and had to grab a second bagel. (he's always eating in class - as we all are ;)) I let him in the class without a late slip (shhhh). We had been waiting for him to get to class, and of course, as usual, he jumped everywhere with some of his buddies. He texted when he wasn't supposed to do so. Played a game on his iPad instead of writing his journal. He even almost fell asleep but decided to stay 'around' to play a game - it WAS Friday - and of course - there were Timbits - so he also ate - again.

When the second period came around - Cameron changed. He became quiet and focussed. I watched him at a distance as he took out some pictures that his mom and dad had lent him to share with us. He had prepared a PowerPoint with memorials. One slide captured the image of his grandmother and two of her cousins while the other displayed pictures of others who had disappeared. There were bricks from the residential schools beneath the monuments, and he explained everything that he knew - the stories that he heard from his family and his beloved grandmother. He choked up often - as he told us how she had was taken at the age of 5. He recalled how she had said to him that her brother had died in the cold while hiding in the forest. He explained how she had witnessed her best friend beaten to death and how she was secretly buried. He talked about the deplorable abuse. The starvation. The illness. He explained in details and was very calm. "They were so young," he repeated. "They never had a chance. They just came and took them away - and there was nothing that they could have done. She was only FIVE" - he repeated often. Cameron loved his grandmother - and it showed in the way that he honored his memory of her. When he concluded, there wasn't a dry eye in the room. Cameron, the young and immature Grade 9 student who never did class presentations - or fails them all because he's never prepared - had spoken for more than 45 minutes. He had brought us back to a time that we did not - or could not - understand - and had explained it in words that were so simple and vivid that one could not remain still. Not now - not ever. His peers were speechless. There was Cameron - the kid they knew as running around everywhere - Triple-A hockey Cameron. He had just shaken their existence, most profoundly and unexpectedly. I asked him: "What message do you want to share with your classmates?" He answered candidly: "Colour of the skin doesn't matter. We're all the same. I love everybody and everybody should."

When he concluded, I did something which I don't often do in my classroom. I cried - and I was speechless. After a few minutes, as I dried my eyes, I told him that I could not be any prouder of what he had done for us. I hugged him and as he hugged me back - I felt him sigh - deeply - as if he had just realized how profound his message had been and what an honor he had been given to share his family's story. I swear his grandmother was standing behind us - smiling as she watched how he had been such a voice for all those who had disappeared. The Forgotten. The hurt. The dead. Through his words - he had given them some peace - and maybe even found a little of his own. I was never prouder to be his teacher, and I told him so. I think that we became friends forever, at that very moment.

Hours later, as I was writing this – I was still crying. There are moments in my career that have defined me. Some students have held an extraordinary place in my heart and soul. I also believe that the Universe has placed others on my path to learn - and to be able to experience the voice of God and Forgiveness - and in the most unlikely of times. That was such a day - and I will forever be grateful to have had Cameron in two of my classes when on regular days - he's the student. That Friday, things were reversed. We were the students. I heard the lesson - loud and clear.

** Sometimes, the voice of the Old Man comes through the voice of a grade nine student telling us about his grandmother's journey and survival in our Canadian residential schools.

I am honored to know you, Cameron. I will never, ever, forget you.

BENCH MOMENT

"We are all living a personal story, and every story has ups and downs, low points and high points. However, what's important is the theme that structures and guides our individual story.

When your story has positive, life-supporting themes, you have found the key to transformation. Changing your argument is more effective than trying to fix yourself one issue at a time. The most positive themes include lightness, worthiness, self-acceptance, evolution, and love.

Your theme should aim at making you feel good every day. It should open new possibilities. It should give you the optimism that you are being renewed.

Have a beautiful sunny day. Get out there - and change lives - perhaps even yours."

WORDS OF MY FATHER

Yesterday, after I had completed all of my 'Saturday must-do chores,' I decided to head out and visit my Father. He is MY personal 'old man.' This time, his television was on (as it usually is), and we discussed World politics and occurrences, trying to figure out this and that. Of course, most of these things are out of our control, and as one individual, we can feel so helpless in not being able to do anything. His voice of reason and wisdom called out, as it usually does. He tends to panic about his matters (as many great ones out there) but is extremely well rounded and insightful when it comes to worldly matters. He told me: "You know, I'm 84 years old and I will have witnessed many changes in my lifetime, as you will in yours - but perhaps this is one where things 'could' be different if we wake up and work 'together' instead of against each other." He commented on the different leaders and presidents - and how the World at times can be very divided because of politics and religion. He lit up when he told me that he believed that our great nations have an unprecedented opportunity to come together - and to see what happens in the next few hours and days. "As we see our fellow humans suffer, we'll bond. Watch. People from ALL over the World will come in aid to those who need it. It's already being done - it's just that the media that we see tends to focus on the negative. We need to change this - and focus on the good things that are done - make THAT feeling grow - that feeling that we can help - the feeling the WE CAN and ARE changing the World - for the better." He continued by saying: "It's a universal law of physics: ONE

atom in the Universe can influence another at the other spectrum of it...
Imagine that Power? We have it in us to make a lasting difference." He
laughed and told me how it's just like *Star Wars* - the Force and Dark
Sides and that this Universal analogy has always existed. He expressed
how he didn't think that Darkness would ever disappear from our
World - but that together - we can shine so much light that it may just
be dimmed enough to make that difference.

Moreover, I smiled. I had just told the same thing to my students on
Friday. Little grade 9 students - our future generation - you know - the
one that we hear doesn't get it? Well - I beg to differ ... These kids one
day will change the world - Heck - they're doing it right now - and they
don't even realize it.

So why am I telling you this - sharing my conversation with my
Father? ... Because I believe that it matters. If only ONE person makes
ONE small gesture - it does make a difference and changes someone's
World. I know it's not new: *The Pay it Forward movement* - but what
if starting today, we DELIBERATELY thought about it - and DID
something about it. One small act of kindness for a family member,
a friend or a total stranger. What if it DID matter - that we tried and
went out of our way to do so - without searching for any recognition
or accolades? IMAGINE power? IMAGINE the change?

Turns out, my impromptu visit with my Father yesterday not only did
change my day - but it may help improve the World. That's something
to smile about.

Sometimes, the Old Man comes through my Father who gently reminds
me that I can and am making a difference in the World.

Shine bright today: *It's a beautiful day.* Xo.

ON LETTING IN THE LIGHT

There is much negativity in our World these days. More than usual, some will even say, and yet I wonder if that's true - or if our thirst for constant news feeds and wanting to know everything is part of it. It's 'funny' how things work: the more we focus on negativity, the more it seems to find us. We find ourselves getting very angry, sad and often spin out of control at things that before would have never affected us in this way. Is it because the World has changed, or because we're changing, and not focussing on what should be our part of particular journeys?

I often feel SO helpless and meaningless in a Universe that seems to be filling itself more with hatred, jealousy, envy, and shame. Too often I think to myself: we're doomed. How are we going to get out of this one, this time ...? Then my Guides, Heavenly and Earth ones, bring me back to my senses and tell me to spread my wings. Spread my light and my smile. That is focussing on one person at a time is the way to be, and that eventually reaches the people we are meant to achieve. I can't help everybody, but I can help someone. Sometimes I can only afford the energy to help myself or those in my close inner circles - but it counts. It's about kindness. Understanding. Patience and Empathy. People don't want to be judged - they want to be understood. So, I try to do that - a person at a time - a moment at a time.

Today, take a moment. Breathe and look around you. You can't change THE world, but perhaps you can change something in somebody's world to make THEIR world better.

Message from the Old Man: *"Love always prevails. Always. Always has. Always will. Here. Then. Tomorrow. Through Multiverses and Time: Love will ALWAYS prevail."*

ABOUT WELCOMING SPRING

I smiled dreamily last night as I took a picture of the view outside my outside window. Winter has been long - but Spring has sprung and is bringing all of her Hope and Abundance with her. Last night, as I was headed out for an early night of sleep in the bunkie, I heard the frogs sing for the first time this year - the sweet melody of Nature, assuring me that Life always finds her flow if you remain patient and keep your faith. It's an analogy for life. Every effort deserves a stamp of approval.

Message from the Old Man: *"Today is full of moments and possibilities for you to love with all of your heart. Live in the Moment. Be original. Always be fearless".*

ABOUT SIMPLE MOMENTS OF SELF-REALIZATION

I know that it will sound like a 'cliché' - but that's ok. I spent the night with THE Old Man on the Bench. True story. This is what ** sleeping on it** often represents for me. At times, there will be many voices within certain situations which will all speak at once - and He is always there to calm them - to eliminate the unwanted ones - and to bring me back to where I should be. I also spent some time with my characters from my novel - heard what 'they' had to say about coming to this realm and sharing their stories to the world. Finally - I woke up and found this quote waiting for me - as well as to another email filled with yet other incredible possibilities. I'm smiling as I realize that I am well-guided by my A-Team and by The Old Man. Life happens when you quiet down and merely listen to the answers that the wind whispers through the branches of a tree.

I spent the night in quiet solitude. Sometimes, as blessed as we are to be alive - it's hard to handle the sudden tragic loss of the ones we love. May everyone remain strong. Tomorrow is another day.

Bench Moment: *"Live passionately. Make a difference. Do your best and choose to shine while remaining authentic. Always try to find joy in ordinary moments".*

Remember this on today's journey: not everyone is on the exact path as you are. It's ok to have differences and not agree. It's okay to feel lost, at times, and to choose to walk away from those who can perhaps ignite deep feelings of 'dissatisfaction.' However, never forget that we can only grow to be better human beings if we surround ourselves, at times, with 'un kindred' minds - so that when we come back to ourselves, we can re-center and focus on what remains essential. Onwards.

If you close your eyes, you will feel it that much stronger today as the country unites with colors of green and yellow: the pulse of a nation, grieving for its own, sending shockwaves of love to those who need it most. We are strong. Love transcends time, distance and reaches hearts in need of healing. Always. xo"

Message from the Old Man: *"Understand that everybody has choices to make and that you cannot be the one who controls their actions except for your own. If you find yourself neglecting your journey, you are missing out on the gift of Life. Stop. Breathe. Remind yourself of your passions and of what makes you fully vibrate and then do more of that. Plan if you must but stop snuffing out your light so that you can please others and fit the imposed box of societal demands. Be kind. Be just. Be you."*

ABOUT SAYING GOODBYE
TO MY FATHER

On June 3d 2018, at precisely 7h44 pm, my Father transitioned to the Light. My brother and I were by his side to share in this inspiring moment for him. You see, my father was no ordinary human being: to those who knew him, he was one of those Earth Angels who touched many individuals on his passage, whether it be with a little note or a simple smile. As his daughter, I am broken, yet I rejoice in the fact that he left EXACTLY on his terms... My mother and himself got to visit one last time yesterday afternoon and as Universe often plays her moments - Maman recognized him and us. She spoke to us. She cried as she saw him and then, a few moments later, made us laugh. They physically touched each other and reconnected as the young lovers they had once been. One day soon, I'll write about it - but that's a future story - for a future moment. Later in the afternoon, we listened to Bob Seger's Against the Wind and Gregorian chants - it was a scene out of a tale of Royals: fitting for a man who taught us how to laugh, how to live and how to love. For now, I would love to extend, on behalf of all my family, extreme gratitude to those who held our space in the past few months. To my family - I will have messages of wisdom to share from the Old Man himself - Ti-Loup. For my family and friends who held my heart with messages and thoughts - I shall never forget you... He held all of you in such high regards: Together, we'll remember him and smile - and we'll honor his memory. As I watched him take his last breath, I smiled. How incredible is it to have your very own Father - now himself a Light Being, share his final transition with you so that one day you can help others: a final gift that my brother and I shall cherish forever. I smile again as I hear him tell me on Saturday morning: "What a beautiful day" ... Look around you everyone - it IS a beautiful day. Je t'aime Papa. Xo

---

Message from the Old Man: *"Soul connections are created at a Universal level and transcend Time and Distance."*

ABOUT TAKING TIME TO HONOUR MY FATHER

Last night, after running around all day for different things, I spent the night in my beloved River House bunkie. It had been a day for getting things done. My Father recently transitioned to the Light on Sunday night. He did so with grace, peace and yes, with a smile. As I lay in bed, it occurred to me how ridiculous things are in our part of the World. Here we are, pure humans - part of a very rushed society, chasing this - jumping for that. Just a few hours ago, I had lost that one person whom I had loved all of my Life: the person who for 48 years listened to my every dream, shaped my way of thinking, loved me for who I was and molded me to become the person that I am today. I didn't even get the chance to sit down, shed a few tears and have a drink in his honor. I didn't get the time to smile, mourn and even think about him. Nope - society dictates that we have so many hours to do this - there is no time for emotions - as we have to go through the 'motions' ... of death.

It bothered me last night. I was saddened, but more pissed that things are the way that they are. A man had just taken his last breath - and here we were, packing up his stuff in boxes because, in so many hours, the cycle continues for another family. I have LISTS of things to do - register for this - send that off - fill this form and answer these questions ... however, nowhere on that list is it written to take the time to stop, take a few hours or a few days and sit still - in silence - and listen to the voices of the Universe whispering to you that things are ok - that you will move on - albeit in a different way.

Of course, I went to sleep holding these thoughts with me. I was exhausted from the day (because I had gone through many of the expected 'lists'), and frustrated because I didn't feel that many around me understand fully how it was for my Father to transition - how it wasn't a sad moment for him - how he had accomplished 'his mission', just as he said that he would. The whole mystery of death to many around me seems sad and final, while He is now smiling - soaring amongst his stars and floating in the wind.

If you know me - the next few sentences will not surprise you. I took those thoughts with me and yes - I found the bench. Guess who was sitting on it ...? You know it - MY Old Man himself - not THE Old Man - but my Father - waiting for me. In true Papa style, he had his drawing pad, a glowing black pen and was staring at the waters. I didn't go very far to see him on this bench - we sat by the River, at my house - on a seat that doesn't yet sit there but will someday soon. When I saw him, he smiled and said: "Allo toute petite. How's everyone doing?" I smiled and wondered why he was even asking - since now he knows everything. He laughed when I didn't answer him. I told him about what had been bothering me - how people just run around and don't take the time to STOP and HONOUR the memories and passing of someone. How many see death as the final step and never quite get over it. I went on and on about this and that ... and in true Papa style, he just sat there in silence, listening to me rant. I don't know what he was drawing - his paper pad was too bright for me to see, but he did tell me that soon he would share what it was - just not yet. As he drew, he told me this: "Time and Wisdom are eternal. When we are on Earth, we are drops in the vast bucket of Eternity. Some understand this now - others may never, and it's not your journey to comment or judge."

"Just do what you do. Play music. Read. Teach your little students about LIFE and take care of your heart. Always - always follow your heart. Of course - write this down and put it in a future book - take my journals and share them with the world. Maybe we'll help one person. Don't worry about what others think. As for running around and not taking time to think about me? Toute p'tite - arrête de t'inquiéter avec ça ... That's PEANUTS. » He chuckled.

I sat there, not speaking for a while and it hit me. *Time and Wisdom are Eternal.* I realized how lucky I am and blessed to 'hear' and 'sense' things that others may not, yet. I now understood, through the words of my Father, that there is no 'correct' way to process things - to mourn and move on - other than the one for ourselves. I've shed tears in the past few days - yet my heart has never felt fuller nor more complete than it does now. My Father is now whole again, flying freely in the Cosmos in which he yearned to return to for years - and he's inspiring me to fly higher. He's giving me things to think about which I never even considered. He's guiding me to live out my passions - in true grace and authenticity. I see that. I feel that, and more importantly, I *know* that.

Before I left the bench to return to this plane, my dad looked over and smiled again. He told me once again: "Arrête de t'inquiéter (stop worrying). Do what you have to do - and then he cited one of his Kenny Rogers songs: there'll be enough for counting - when the dealing's done." He laughed again. He told me a few more personal things which I shall keep for myself at the moment, and then he told me that he had things to do and would talk to me later - then he vanished. I sat there for a few extra minutes and just smiled. I know now that running around is part of our 'reality' - and that's ok. More importantly, I now have a 'direction' for a new project that I've been working on for months - about Holding Space for myself and Others - and I have the needed material to pen yet another book about the Old Man on the Bench - Wisdom from MY Old Man ... So today, I'll go through the lists. Sign this paper. Read this passage and smile. After all, it's just peanuts. Later on, I'll sit still, grab a pen and a little notebook and I'll start writing. I'll listen to the songs of the birds, I'll smell the air of wonder, and I'll watch the leaves moving in the Wind and think of my Father.

Message from MY Old Man: *"I have become the Wind ... my song is just beginning"... What a beautiful day. Xo*

ABOUT MEETING THE OLD MAN IN AN OLD CHURCH

Recently, when I visited Paris, I did something which I had not done in years. I walked into one of the oldest churches in Paris, Ste Sulpice, expecting to visit and admire the old architecture. I was to light a few candles, pay my respects and then quickly leave. Of course, the Universe had other plans, and something bigger happened: I healed my Spirit.

I'm not going to give you many details, for some things are best left unsaid. Suffice it to say that for many years now, I have held many burdens in my heart - both for myself and for others. Although I am blessed to have Guides with me at all times, I could no longer hear and feel them as loudly as before - which saddened and preoccupied me - for I know that my true calling is only beginning. I was tired. I felt lost. I was currently unable, and I had no idea how I was to rekindle this light and energy. Then I looked around. There, in the corner of this grandiose church which has stood in Paris since the 1660s, was a small meeting place where people could go and speak to the Monsignor. I walked around the church ... and was led back, although reluctantly, to wait for him. I sat right next to the cross on the floor (you know the one you see in the Da Vinci Code?) - and the sun shined on it. I observed multitudes of people visiting the church - walking past us - the ones who waited - while others joined me on the little small rattan chairs next to his 'cubicle.' I had no idea why I waited - I didn't want to say anything - certainly, a confession was not my 'forte' ... and I was about to meet a total stranger in a familiar, yet foreign city. Then things became very quiet and around me, and the energies shifted. The Universe opened up, and I was able to see a cool blue light entering the area around me, and at that moment, the door to the priest's cubicle opened. I 'saw' myself walking in and sitting down in front of him - not knowing what would come of this 'meeting.' After he introduced himself, he looked at me and asked what he could do to help me. I smiled - I could write NOVELS about what he could do to help me yet I was very honest with him - and I shared (amongst other things) that at times, I found life to be such a burden - that it's sometimes incredibly difficult to be strong for others - as I see myself falling apart. I shared a few stories. I shared many intimate details, and then I looked at him. He was smiling and looking 'around' me - telling me not to worry: that I had a 'team' of angels and guides surrounding me. Although I was only human in form, I was Universal in spirit - that although I want to help everyone, I can't but that I can help 'someone' along with my journeys. At that moment, I wasn't speaking with the 'priest' himself - but with the Universal Force which guides us all - no matter what we choose to call it. Some may say that it is God, others the Love source, while others may call it Father-Mother. It doesn't matter - what does matter is the incredible healing energy coming from that source. I listened with intent to what he had to say. Then, as he blessed me, I felt re-energized with light and patience - and felt ready to go about my day - and about my life journey. I smiled as I walked out. I had just sat down 'ON' a bench - with an Old Man ... a concrete personification of THE Old Man from the book had transpired. In an old church. IN Paris - the city which has held my heart and spirit for many lifetimes. It was a beautiful and poetic moment - one I that I will hold on to for many more years to come. More than one hour had passed. His other 'meetings' had been about 10 minutes long. I took that as a vital sign.

I'm home now - and one may wonder if that feeling is still within me ... The answer is yes. Many things have changed - but the feeling I had when I exited his cubicle remains. In the past few days, I've noticed how things 'sound' different. The colors are brighter. Sounds are more apparent, and although I am still dazed from the jet-lag, things have become clear again. I smile. I think that I spoke to God on that morning and that all my Guides were in there with Him - cheering me on - and reassuring me that I was exactly where I am supposed to be - at this very moment - in my present adventures.

That said - I'm ready: ready to accept that I am not perfect and that I often lose my temper. That I say things that I regret because I am so impulsive - yet try to make amends. I understand that I was given the gift of 'hearing' and 'sensing' - to help others while becoming myself a better human being. Not a 'perfect' human being - but one who does the best that she can under particular circumstances. What more can I ask for?

If you're looking for me - or want to talk to me about this - please send me a private message. I'll answer you back for sure. In the meantime, I'll be out there living Life - doing this and that ... and I'll smile and remember that I'm lucky to be alive and surrounded by all these graces and mysteries.

Bench Moment: *Today, I bought some extraordinary items today - made by my little neighbors. Scrunchies. They were selling them on the side of the road: ** We went to Ottawa and saw people with no money. When we go back - we're giving them the money we get from selling these. ** My heart grew a million sizes bigger. How special is that?*

** Last night, it rained. Mother Nature cleared away all of the clouds during the night to make this a perfect morning to which to wake up. There are universal messages of hope if you take a moment to look out your windows. Here is what was right outside my River House this morning.

Bench Moment: *"Attitude is everything. Live in the moment. Embrace the journey. Hold on tight and pretend it's the plan because it may have been all along"* …

ABOUT LIFE AND HER MYSTERIOUS CIRCLES

I had an interesting conversation with my husband the other night ... About 'Life' and her circles. You know - the kind of stuff that's 'easy' to handle after a long day at work. (insert smile here). Many of the people I met and became friends with when I was just four years old are still a significant part of my current and daily life. Some friends disappeared for years, others for a brief moment - yet, in true Universal serendipity - they're the connections that were meant to be and that have helped forge whom I have become - and many have resurfaced in the past few years. We all seem to be reconnecting at this time of our journeys.

Some of these individuals have become colleagues. Another has become my supervisor. Some had their lives lost to car accidents when they were only teenagers (but thanks to being neighbors with their family, and my natural capacities - I've reconnected with them - and have managed to have them also do so with their loved ones). A few nearly bit the bullet: cancer, heart attacks, and brain injuries, depression ... Others have lost children - parents - spouses. I now teach some of their children and have become friends with a few of them: an extension of their parents who are so very dear to me - in person and Spirit. You know - the kind of stuff that's hard to handle and that make you appreciate the rays of sunshine when they do appear variety of life-altering events: I've witnessed these friends' dark moments and have been fortunate enough to help a few (and still am - I hope) go through unspeakable difficult moments. We're still holding space for each other now - as we did so many years ago when we were growing up, feeling alone and lost. We again trust each other - in our connections - in our joys and sorrows - in our conversations and our silence.

At almost 49 years old and what seems like a lifetime of experiences, I smile and think how incredible this journey has been so far. Growing up, I was that very odd child. I was intuitive. Cute (ah ah). Artistic and very socially 'strange.' I had autism, of course (...) and could tell people of things I heard and saw that would happen. Many laughed. Many others didn't. I was attracted to the troubled souls. The sad. The lonely. I easily became friends with them - as maybe they were a reflection of who I was, at that moment. Many of these people are still around me, within my heart and soul, to this very day. It finally really clicked how brilliant the Universe's plan for my life truly is. Through the 'coincidental' meetings of people on our journeys, we create dynamic synergy and are bound to interact which each other - whether for a minute or a lifetime. Not all connections will matter - but those that do stay with you have the power to impact your days and years. Here. There. Now. Then.

The real connections that I hold are as strong today as they were rediscovered 44 years ago. (Yep - I believe in past lives - about how our energies live on and how we re-experience each other - life after life ... however, that's a whole different topic for another day) The few girls (and seemingly more abundant boys - typical for Aspie girls by the way) who were there that long ago are still somewhere in the present - intertwined on my journey. They stood by me in high school as I cried myself to sleep - either while sitting with me at band practice or while writing for the school paper. Some left - others stayed and witnessed my Life unfolding before our very eyes: the 'chance' meeting with my husband. They held my space as I journeyed into motherhood - lost - so very lost - and helped me forge ahead on a road which at times seemed impossible to navigate, especially as an adult on the ASD spectrum.

They were present when I was trying to come to grasp that I was an intuitive reader and fell to the floor, literally in a fetal position, and cried for days. They helped me claw myself out of dark moments when I nearly lost my father to heart disease, my brother to a debilitating stroke and as I still struggle the internal conflict of my relationship with my mother who has Alzheimer's. I have connected with my parents' friends whom, growing up, were a solid part of my daily travels - and have become entwined with them. They are now amongst my closest soulmates and friendships. My brother's best friends down south now hold special places in my soul as I rediscovered soul sisters - who held me as I fell - and are very much present in my life today ... They also lost loved ones and are dealing with incredible challenges. They have their stories - but because of my own 'circle' - I've now become part of theirs and on THEIR journey with them ... Another drew the cover of my book series: The Old Man on the Bench - the very same one whom I met when I was in grade 5, and that told me the first time that he saw me that he had never seen anyone with such bright hair.

My children have transformed themselves to be my best friends and allies and thanks to this - I've found the love and beauty of individuals I would have never met had it not been for them. See? It's about connections - how we should honor them and live them fully while we are here - now - in this very moment. There are those who will not understand: why her? Him? Now? Then? They will not grasp the purpose nor the reasons - but it matters not. If you listen with your heart and you become attuned to that universal 'connective' language, it won't matter. You know. They know. The Universe knows, and that's all which will matter. It's all that SHOULD matter ...

Not everybody will be everything to one person. Some people will be innocent bystanders in your Life. Some will be here for a moment while many will transcend with you throughout all of your moments. Some will become parents, children, life-partners, lovers, a best friend, a soulmate or a colleague. All will bring something magical to your Life - if you pay attention and you allow yourself to savor the blessings that they bring forth to your existence, you will become the wealthiest person in the Universe. Think about it. It's simple.

To all the many people of my Life circle, I honor your presence. Thank you for being part of my lifetimes. I loved you then, now and will forever: such is the power of Life, of Love and mysterious Circles. *Namaste.*

Message from the Old Man: *"Offer what you desire and let all who judge you stay where they are."*

** It was an ordinary Saturday, filled with magical moments. I spent time outside, followed the flow of Life and smiled as I encountered simple moments. It doesn't have to be complicated you know. If you open your heart, you hear the voice of the Universe whispering to you.

ABOUT SPENDING FATHER'S DAY WITHOUT MY PAPA

Dear Papa,

This will be the very first Father's Day that I will not have you in my life, to hug and to kiss on the cheek. There will be well-wishers and friends sending me advice, comforting words and advice on how to navigate this tough day and I'll smile as I accept their love ... however, it won't bring you back - it won't let me hug you and tell you about how I find the world is ridiculous - and wait for the comfort of your words and wisdom.

It's occurred to me in the past few weeks that the World revolves around us - and I mean that generically: humans worry about themselves, about their survival and journeys. Although my world stopped dead in its tracks - if I look around me, I'll notice that deadlines still happen, people always walk, eat and work. It's like I'm observing the World from the inside out - looking in - and at times - I don't even want to rejoin that bubble they're all in. I see them running, getting angry and frustrated. They're missing the point - I'd tell you - Life is not about running around all the time - Life is about following your inner callings and honoring your truths. I smile as I hear you telling me just a few weeks ago: "ALWAYS follow your heart ..." Easy words to mutter - not as easy to live, as you well know.

Last night, I spent the night in my renovated retro Nook. You, perhaps more than others, will remember how at just seven years old, I told you that one day I would own an old 'Boler' - in my backyard and that I would sleep there - alone - and enjoy the sounds of Nature as I woke up. I smiled again this morning as I woke up and thought about how you'd think this place is perfect: a retreat for the artist and writer in me – patiently waiting and yearning to emerge. A place for the dreamer that I am. For the time-traveler that I love being. To become whole again. To become more like you were - to follow my own heart. I almost called you on the way home last night - I was bursting to tell you about how it was going to be 'THE' night - but I forgot that you wouldn't be answering the phone when I called ... A few silent tears fell, and then I took a deep breath and remembered that I'm one of the lucky ones. I talk to people in Spirit - and then once again, I smiled.

I remember that Heaven DOES have a phone and that you answer, every single time that I have called. In the past two weeks, I've found 19 random dimes — a loonie. Countless messages and signs that you're around me - stronger than ever in fact - for you no longer live in the frail body which held your incredible soul. You flow freely now - through the leaves of trees and in the wind. You've become part of the current of the river - and your voice has never been stronger. You and I have always shared core beliefs about Life and the Universe. One day, we'll share with the World what we believe - and why resilience seems to be part of our father-daughter essence. The time is not quite right - the moment has not arrived - for, as your little girl - I am still processing the fact that although I am with you in Spirit, you are not around for me to touch and feel ... I'm still processing the fact that tomorrow, I won't be able to bring you a Father's Day card ... and that you won't kiss the top of my head as you always do.

I'm crying right now - but I won't be all day - I know you hate it when I complain. Instead, I'll share this note with people - to tell them that they're not alone either - should they be missing 'their' daddy. I know that Bill's dad is there too - and that he'll be crying as well - after all - you two gentlemen were in a class of your own - and this is the first year that neither of you will be around tomorrow for Father's Day. I don't know how to do this: I don't know how to navigate this but what I DO know is this: I'll make you proud. I know you'll show up somehow, somewhere ... I know that my A-Team will hold my heart as I journey into the unknown ... I am strong. I am brave, and I am your daughter. Just like in the Lion King - remember that scene when Simba misses his dad? He looks deeper, and Rafiki, your favorite character - tells him: "Look closer: he lives in YOU" ... So, enough crying - let's show them how to do this also - with class.

Je t'aime Papa ... (and I would love to hold you just one. last. time.)

Xo

Message from the Old Man: *"Feel how memories mark your Soul. Repeat after me: My heart heals my life."*

ON TAKING A HEALING ME DAY

When I opened my eyes this morning, I knew that this was THE day. Although I could 'see' and 'hear' what was around me, I didn't want to be in this moment. I had been wandering the streets of Dreamland just a few minutes ago, with no real objective except to avoid being 'here' - and when the time came to 'wake up,' I didn't - no - let me rephrase that, I couldn't do it. I, however, managed to do so after a few minutes and decided that today, I needed to hold my own space. I couldn't see anyone. Talk to anyone. Interact with anyone. I saw myself getting some work ready for my ever-so-patient-and-understanding students - and then I crashed into my office chair. Stoned it seemed - but not from a drug I had ingested, but rather from the enormous crash of Life which appeared to have made its touchdown while I slept. I had choices: move on - or let time take its course. Wait out as the emotions journeyed in front of my eyes - one by one - like a parade of uncoordinated dance moves in a routine that still requires rehearsal or force myself to be the healthy, expected person that I usually am. This morning, I allowed myself to be a witness to myself, to the moments which had occurred in the past few months and few days - and I chose to embrace all of the rawness, difficulty, and beauty that they had brought forth in my current journey.

Those who know me - genuinely know me - understand that I am often an enigma to myself. I am *a mystic*, they say. I see things, sense things and can connect with those in Spirit. (Believe or not - I am not here to convince you - I am stating who I honestly am). I travel through time. I remember lives and times in which I walked through - then I am a person who is probably one of the more flexible ones, you will say. I know what to say. I understand silence. I am present for others in mind and spirit if they require me to do so. I wear and hold many hats and many hearts, and am forever grateful to those who allow me to witness their timelines - and include me in theirs. However, sometimes, I also forget that I am human and that I too need to let things be - that I too need to experience that large gamma of emotions. Yes, I am connected to the Universe, as we all are, of course - but sometimes, I also need to be reminded that although I am special - I am just that - *special like everyone else*. There are no real differences between us - and when one of us loses or grieves, the moments come. I, just like others, need to take that moment at being silent. Observe the thoughts. Honor the memories. Cry the tears and finally let go.

So, I sent in my work. I then sat back in my office chair in the Paris room, found some music on YouTube - put on my headphones, and I pressed play. The first song sang its opening notes. I was still numb. The next melody then played, and something stirred within me - yet nothing. I finally found a song by The Script - and bingo. There they were. Tears: flowing freely down my cheeks. I cried for this. I cried for that. I cried for him and her. I cried for my family and friends. So then I cried for myself. Soul-cleansing, heart-cleansing, knowing it's going to be ok tears. I waited for the moment to pass ... and it finally did.

About an hour later, I was finally able to walk to the kitchen, make myself some breakfast and wash it down with some coffee. I didn't taste any of the food - yet I knew that I needed substance to get moving. After sitting some more in office, it came. The energy that I had waited for suddenly appeared - and it filled me with hope, life, and love. Today - the Universe sent me a beautiful young girl in Spirit - gorgeous black eyes and impeccable French accent - and she reminded me in perfect Parisian français that life goes on - I am loved, and it's all that mattered at that moment.

I smiled and thanked her. I love this young lady (one day - perhaps - I'll introduce you to her but the time has not yet come to do so. She may, after all, only be a figment of my imagination ;)). I got up and decided that it was time to shake off the remainder of this energy. I showered. I got dressed and put on my makeup. As I was applying my favorite shade of lipstick, I glanced up in the mirror, and there she was, standing to my right, smiling at me with her gorgeous red lips and I knew that I was going to be okay. I had a moment - I needed a moment - I had honored myself and my memories, and I could finally move on.

Should you find yourself in a similar situation - remember - Life goes on. However, it would be best if you also honored yourself and everything that goes with whatever situation you may be experiencing. Sleep. Eat. Cry if you must. Take a vacation from Life and people and be with yourself for a few hours or a few days. It's okay. Life is right - the Universe is, and so are you. Remember that - always. I know that today was the best decision that I could have made for myself. I am now off to enjoy the rest of this healing day. What a beautiful day.

Bench Moment: *"Always keep some room in your heart for the unimaginable. Life is meant to be a great adventure. Find that ray of sunshine as you live. Be amazed and embrace your daily journey. Own your dreams and be brave."*

ON FALLING APART
WHILE HEALING

When I embarked on my healing journey, I promised you that I would keep you updated. After all, I am an intuitive person, a teacher and a coach who helps people along their journeys ... so it's interesting to 'know' what transpires ... right? The truth is - I had a very shitty day. I miss my ear. My confidant. My person. I miss my Papa. I needed to talk to him today - and found myself dialing his phone number. Again. I hung up - and I shut down. I know he hears me. I know he's around me. However, tonight, I am that daughter who just happened to land on one of his emails and forgot temporarily that he was gone from this plane - forever. What I'm about to write will likely shock you - but there will be language. This fk**ing sucks. Off I go to bed to try and sleep off this day. Tomorrow is, after all, another day. This too shall pass - I will keep looking up.

ABOUT THIS MOMENT
CALLED LIFE

Something occurred to me yesterday as I was attempting to teach my Grade 10 students. Keyword: trying. It was Friday afternoon. They had a group task to do - and of course - I let them partner up themselves. As I observed the individuals with whom they chose to work with, I smiled, and I was sent back 30 years into time, at a moment when my teachers used to do the same for us. I think that these individuals were very intuitive. They, just as I do now, 'knew' who would be with whom and they didn't seem to care. The truth is, I always landed with the same people. There was the one who drew. The one who tapped his pen and then one who just socialized and bugged us and made us laugh until we cried. Then there were us, two girls who did all the work - did the corrections and submitted it - as a group - and of course - got an excellent mark. While at the time the mark DID matter - the truth is - it never really did - because it wasn't meant to do so. You see, I think that my teachers were brilliant human beings who allowed us to work together only to get to know each other, learn to tolerate each other and often allowed us to become lifelong friends. Bonds like these are impossible to form in a short period - and so as high school progressed - I was fortunate to have five solid years with many of these individuals - and we are still incredible friends today.

Over the years, we lost some of these people. Some took their own lives when Life became too hard to tolerate. Others lost their partners. Some had heart attacks and survived - while others fought the battle of their lives and came out victorious over diseases too dark to even mention. However, through it all, and all because we worked in groups in high school and didn't accomplish much - we were able to 'be' together and help each other through the darkest of times. Funny how you never think about that until the Universe gently taps you on the head at 14h11 on snowy Friday afternoon. I smile this morning as I think about all the memories. I laugh as I still hear the jokes - as I see one of them escape through the window during a fire drill - and as other draws on the corner of my sheets. I see the smiles of ones, I feel the comfort in others, and I thank the Universe that my teachers had the 'ability' to 'know' .... and just let us be. We all eventually learned how to spell. Grammar didn't matter. A crooked picture and a misquote were never important ... What WAS important were the connections that we made, that grew into love and friendship - and how we still have those today.

Bench Moment: *"If we don't allow people to create memories - they will never remember the important moments."*

ABOUT MEETING THE
OLD MAN IN A CAB

Yesterday, I came back from Toronto. I spent some time at the airport. I had time to think - reflect and process. I made plans for the next few weeks - imagined the future months and asked the Universe to help me organize the forthcoming years. I think that I was very successful at it - sometimes, a little break is what one needs to put things into perspective... It never fails - at least in my case - when Life becomes somewhat confusing and 'mundane,' the Universe sends me signs, messages if you will, through the most unlikely of persons. Of course, it happened again - this time, when I was returning to the hotel after my meeting on Friday. Suzanne, the young lady organizing the webinar had called cabs to bring us back to our different destinations - and I decided that I would take the first one to arrive. As I made my way to the cab and waved goodbye to my colleagues, I heard the Universe whisper. It came more like a gentle flutter, but I knew that I would meet someone 'interesting,'

Of course, my A-Team did not disappoint. This time, the Old Man came through the voice of Paul, from *Pakistan* - he insisted - and my 45 minutes ride to the hotel thus began. I knew He was someone special because when I walked into the cab, he shook my hand and I felt an energy like no other. I knew it was time to listen - and so I did. I learned about why he had chosen Canada as his new home. He told me about his Masters in Economics and showed me pictures of his family. He was very proud - so well spoken - so gentle and so wise. We then shifted our focus on me. What did I do? Where did I live? He jotted down the information for Santa's Village for his little 6-year-old boy - and asked questions about the best time to visit to see the maples switch colors. In the end, I told him that I was a teacher - like his wife - He said - and that I had written a small book and was working on two others. "I want to be an author," I told him. "I want to travel - speak - and inspire people." He smiled and told me this: "If you put it out there - all your dreams come true, Anne." (side note - I had NOT told him my name). He then told me this: "It's crucial to time stamp things in this dimension because Time doesn't exist in the universal dimensions." Then he looked up, smiled - and we pulled up to the hotel.

When I walked out of his cab, I was smiling - as he was. We exchanged the fare and then he told me how I should never forget that the Universe hears everything - and to use its power. "It is - after all - what I do every day, and I am delighted", he said. I smiled and shook his hand - again. Same energy - but this time I swear that his eyes were shiny and laughing - even more alive, if you will. I watched him drive away. I had learned quite the lesson - and intended to put it to the test. I asked for one last sign - looked down - and found a dime. Yep - out of nowhere - at my feet - a dime. I smiled and picked it up. There it was - again - the sign that I had asked for - validation for what had just happened.

Later that night, I was still smiling. Things had become more evident and as I put my intentions in the Universe - I knew that She had heard me. I marveled about how lucky I am - to be living where I am - in my beautiful community - by the River - no less. I counted my incredible blessings: my family, my friends, my colleagues and my students who make me smile every day. Life is not always perfect - but it is weaved with perfect moments - sometimes, you need someone like Paul to remind you of what matters in Life.

Sometimes, the voice of the Old Man comes through that of a Toronto cab driver, reminding you about what matters in life and how your dreams can come true if you believe in them.

Thanks, Old Man. I received the message - loud and clear. Xo

Message from the Old Man: *"Always believe in the good of people."*

ON THE PASSAGE OF TIME

It came late at night – and unexpectedly. I was enjoying a vacation in the Canadian Rockies with my family when I heard the distinctive sound of a text message coming through. It was from a high school friend who had heard about my Father's passing, and he was extending his sympathies to my family and I. I was startled. He was for sure the last person I had planned on hearing from, especially now – so far away from home – and because of various circumstances. Time had left a big gap between our lives, and it seemed that even though I was always curious to find out about his latest adventures, I had never gotten around to catching up with him. Like Phil Collins said in his song: there was always something more important to say, more important to do. We chatted here and there and became slowly reacquainted. He found out about my 'exploits,' and I caught up with his undertakings. Life had been brutal in many ways for both of us on a personal level, yet, strong as we were, we always found a way to get through the next adventures and to successfully move on. He told me about his family: his beautiful wife, his three children, and his business ventures. Though more than 30 years had passed, Time had somehow managed to stand still, and the light-hearted shy blonde guy I had met in high school, who explained my math homework and for whom I corrected spelling mistakes was still very much the same at heart. He longed to make his family happy and to care for the ones whom he loved. He was still searching for the bigger meaning of Life and had never yet witnessed it, it seemed. I found out that he had lost his father to cancer, and that his mother, whom I knew very well, was doing well and living next door to his house. Later that Summer, his father in law became very ill. His wife and daughter came down to visit with him, and his 15-year-old teenager was suddenly (and so very) bored. Late at night, another ding came out of nowhere: could I PLEASE take his daughter out to lunch and occupy her for a day? Change her mindset? Perhaps refocus on things in a different light? It wasn't a decision I took very lightly. After all, I had not seen him in more than three decades, and yet there he was, asking me, a most antisocial person, to entertain a young woman about whom I knew nothing... I agreed (reluctantly). We met 'online' so that at least I knew who she was beforehand. Wednesday morning, as we had agreed by numerous texts with her mother, I drove out to the local coffee house, met Mom and Daughter – assured her that she was in good hands – me – a total stranger and that I would have her daughter back by 6 pm that evening. She seemed nervous, but also almost relieved that for a few hours, I would take her daughter's mind off serious things – things too difficult for even a seasoned adult to comprehend. True to my promise, I took care of my friend's daughter. After a pedicure and food, Dominique and I went on the carousel, went shopping and talked about Life. She told me stories about herself, about her father and giggled a lot. She's not different from most teenagers: she is young, fresh and certainly stunning. Her blue eyes articulate wisdom brought on by reading, thinking and pondering about her life journey. She, like all of them, has qualms about her parents, has crushes that are meant to remain secret FOREVER, she loves too much, has a vision of what life could be and still doesn't know what she wants to be 'when she grows up.' As I sat in the car and we listened to music, I recognized her father's wit and humor – she was, after the all, the same age that he had been when we first met. I smiled as she found the same things which he had so many years ago - funny. I laughed when I saw that unimportant events tick her off – just like they had also ticked him off. Through it all, as I got to know her better, I rediscovered THROUGH her, my friendship with her father and I realized this: soul connections transcend time and distance, and nothing can break that bond once it tethers you together. I smiled as I spoke with him – and I realized this important fact: he had lent me, for the day, his most precious person: his daughter. He had given me the opportunity to connect back with him, through her – and had given me the chance to witness what kind of person HE had become in Life, through the person of his child. I smiled again as I spoke with the Universe. Life is indeed serendipitous. It didn't always show itself in obvious ways, but Fate has an idea of reuniting those who belong in shared circles, whether it be 30 minutes, 30 days or 30 years later. True story.

Bench Moment: *"Time sits still. True friends may not hear from each other in years and in no time at all, it's like they were never apart."*

Power Song time on a Friday. I'm feeling 'meh' this morning - but this one song always manages to raise my spirits. Music is magical. Put headphones on, press play, turn the volume up and repeat, again and again, until I feel that 'whoosh' of energy flow through me. Being alive is a privilege. Being healthy is a gift and having loved ones around me is an honor. I'm not going to waste these gifts because I'm not quite feeling up to par ...

ABOUT THE MEANING
OF TRUE LOVE

Today, my grade 9 students were working on a personal timeline. One of them told me that he had fallen in love when he was in Grade 3. "Does that count?", I asked. "Of course, it does," he answered. "Explain to me what love looks like in Grade 3." "Being in love is sharing your Fruit Snacks with someone, Madame." I then asked him: "How do you know if it's TRUE love?", I replied. "You give her the colors that you love to eat ..."

Bench Moment: *"Accept simple moments of happiness in your life."*

ABOUT HITTING ROCK BOTTOM

On June 3d 2018, at precisely 7:01 pm, my Father transitioned to the Light. It was the night that I temporarily died inside. You may think that I handled it well - for that indeed is the image that I put forth, yet as I was grasping at straws to hold on to my sanity, I had fallen to such depths that really, I didn't know when or if I would ever get out of it. I was now like everyone that had been close to a parent and lost them: I was a child who would have to go through grief - and hopefully, get better as time went on.

I only took one week off work. The end of the school year was near, and it certainly didn't feel like the time to have to explain everything to a supply teacher. So, after going through the motions and legalities of it all - death is quite the business - I was left standing - smile on my face and devastation in my heart. Though family and friends surrounded me, I had never felt so alone and empty. It hurt to walk. Food lost its taste and mind fog had set in. Only then did I start to notice that my heart had broken and that I was headed straight to a sad, cold and dark place.

Contrary to what I had done before in my Life, this time, I let myself go there, in moderation. I knew that I had steps to honor and that it was going to be the most challenging thing that I had done so, to date. I had faced burnout before because of autism, stroke, and Alzheimer - but I had never been to the midst of desperation like I was suffering now. I existed: a moment at a time - a second at a time. All I wanted to do was eat and sleep. People got to me. I lost the glitter in my eyes and the hope in my heart. I had lost my best friend. The man who still held so many of my secrets - the one who had brought me guidance throughout my Life - was now gone. I was alone (or so it seemed). I only vaguely remember the next few months. I know I went to Jasper with my husband and my son - yet I recall nothing much of the trip, except for a few moments and conversations. After almost a year of eating plant-based and sugar-free 'good' food - I revolted against my body and began eating meat and sugar again. I ate in quantities which were out of character for myself - but I didn't care. Many friends reached out to me. Their daily messages saved me. Summer ended (and again - I remember almost none of it) and September reared its face. Again - the last semester passed on without my realizing it. I know that many times, I nearly broke and almost asked to take some time off ... People were constantly finding me - asking me to help 'them' with their issues - and they never seemed to worry about mine. I was tired. Life exhausted me. I didn't care about many things - I was sinking and fast. I decided to set myself some goals: walking my grief away ... I walked a million steps in 100 days. I reached goals - I succeeded in other forums - but I was still so lost. Grief inhabited me. It comes in waves, they said. Then it will get better. My grief came in tsunami form - and didn't get better. As Christmas approached - I allowed myself to hit rock bottom. On Christmas Day, surrounded by family and dogs - I wailed and cried and silently screamed. I don't remember much of that day either, to tell you the truth - because it was perhaps too painful to deal with things. I allowed myself to feel what I had to feel ... I was in 'liminal' space,' and as Heather Plett had taught me to do, I sat there. I observed. I patiently waited until I saw a glimmer of light. It didn't come that day, nor the next - nor the one after that. I was quietly beginning to feel desperation. Had it not been for the careful and attentive ear of choice few loved ones, I would have fallen into a ravine and gotten very ill .... but fortunately, that did not happen.

On February 4th, 2019, I looked in the mirror, and I woke up. I stirred from what had felt like a bad dream. I looked at myself for the first time in what seemed like months, and I saw what I had become. I looked tired. My eyes were dead, and my skin looked sallow. I tried to wear a pair of pants, and they were too tight. My hands couldn't close, and I noticed that my knees were cracking again. I noticed that my energy was almost gone and that my intuition had all but disappeared. I had become that person whom I often saw coming to ME for help. I had fallen - and it was time to get up. So, I did. I set out a plan - for the next day. I, after all, had done this before. Every day, there would be goals. Plans. Things to do to slowly get better and heal my broken heart, my torn spirit, and my exhausted body. I decided to take things slowly - one moment at a time - and to rebuild myself - again - but this time - better and stronger because I am aware of what needs to be done ...

When One is ready, it doesn't take long to make changes and to feel better, and things have immensely improved in the past few weeks. I am eating plant-based again. I'm listening to music. I'm rebuilding myself - a dull moment at a time and this time, I'm sharing my journey with you - so that you may find inspiration to get through whatever it is that you may need to get through. It's time to put everything I know into action - for myself. So yes - I still miss my Dad and often write: F*** I miss you - and I always will. However, it's time to move forward - He wants and needs me to. I am. It's not easy, but #watchme. I'll do it.

ABOUT SLEEPING THROUGH SEASONS

One of my best friends said something this morning: "It's okay sometimes to sleep through seasons." The truth is - I hadn't been 'present' since June last year. I've existed - but not fully lived. I stopped taking care of myself. No walking. No eating right. Just existing. I had Lost my Mind-Body-Spirit connections. Grief does that to you - and sometimes, all you can do is ride its waves until you're ready to emerge. I think I am ready to get up ... again. Here we go. Again. I'm ready to live now. Again. Step one: journaling and taking care of my health. It's going to be a long road to recovery - but I've got this. Thanks to those who held my back and my heart as I was crashing to what I thought was the bottom. It was there that I rose.

Message from the Old Man: "There will be times in your life when the space between breaths is the only holiday that you'll be able to afford. However, in this space, if you are attentive, you will find the most incredible treasures and moments. Understand that these moments which will save your existence sometimes last only a few seconds. Pay attention, always, or you may miss them."

ABOUT THE NEW YEAR

I have often considered February the start of a new year. Perhaps it is because a new semester at school begins, or that the hope for Spring whispers through the never-ending snow. Regardless of reasons, I always find this time essential to reflect on myself, and to set various personal objectives. This year is no different, but perhaps in my mind's eye, I am more focused and determined in my goals to renew my person: Mind. Body. Spirit. It's time. Old energies and ideologies will vanish. New ones will emerge. Things, moments (and yes - people as well) that no longer bring joy to my heart or allow me to grow positively will be slowly phased out by the elements of Life that do provide those very opportunities to do so. In my studies with Heather Plett, we call this waiting for emergence 'liminal space' ... that quiet contemplation time meant to reflect, observe and wait for what's going to appear. The next few weeks will be just that. I'm standing back - waiting. Breathing. Observing and then taking steps to vibrate at a very different level. Life is good - if you allow it to be. Have a beautiful day - and happy new year!

Bench Moment: *"There are days such as these: you wake up and want to walk away from it all – but only for a day. On such days I close my eyes and retreat to my magical islands in my mind's eye. I sit there for a few minutes, on the bench, until I can breathe in calmness. I feel the images and taste the scents. I'm never alone for I am part of the Universe and we are all connected somehow – somewhere in time ... also, I can't forget that."*

ABOUT LIFE'S SIMPLE MOMENTS

I just stood outside for a few minutes, while coming in from a very epic sleep in the bunkie. It's quiet out there - and the snow clouds have moved away. As I looked around, I marveled at how much snow surrounded me - it was almost like being in another time - and another moment ... Quiet meditations on the seventh day of going back to eating plant-based and of reconnecting myself to what matters to me. Life is about capturing moments and about allowing your imagination to run free, while your Soul shines as bright as it can be. It's a beautiful day.

ABOUT MY DENTIST (AND FACING MY GREATEST FEAR)

We all experience moments which have been life-altering. Some of these are witnessed in close intimate circles, while others are just there, seemingly floating around for us to discover them. This one, in particular, was very evident, but I had missed it for many years because I had become caught up in a loop of fear. You see, growing up, I had to, like every child, go to the dentist's office. Albeit a nice man, I was deathly terrified of mine. For weeks before my appointment, I would be sick. I would cry and have every excuse in the book for not showing up. I still managed to go, and for years – I felt this extreme anxiety whenever I had to make it in. One day, a new dentist moved his practice into our little town. By now I was an adult, capable of making my own decisions. Although I had been fearless and appreciated the other members of our dental community for the help that they had given me, I knew that I had to make a change and so, I bravely walked in and made an appointment for a consultation. I was greeted with a smile, and I landed face to face with some individuals whom I have come to hold dearly in my heart. There was Nathalie, Angèle, Sylvie and of course, the man himself, Dr. Roberge. As I sat in his chair, I explained to him how for years I had cried before going to appointments. I told him how I hated pain, and how I dreaded getting dental work. I had been scared, and I wanted no more. He listened to me, with amusement and compassion in his eyes. He looked at me and just told me: "Don't cry. I won't hurt you." For some reason, I believed him, and the rest is history.

Over the years, I've made numerous visits to his cabinet. Dr. Roberge's team always welcomes me with a smile, and truth be told, I have become very comfortable and feel almost 'at home' when I go there. I've endured a few root canals, fillings, and cleanings. As I speak, I am about to become a 'queen' – waiting to be adorned with two crowns to save my teeth which, once upon a time, decided it was a good idea to bite into a soft Hallowe'en candy. Not only has he managed to save my teeth and ensure that I have a glowing smile for years, but this incredible man has taught me a more important lesson about Life itself. It's okay to be afraid, but if you surround yourself with caring people whom you trust, you're never alone, and you don't have to endure pain. One should take a deep breath – and understand that more challenging moments always pass – they still do. Who knew that one could learn about life in a dental office. Funny how Universe places people on our paths in that of dentists when one least expects it. "Cheese" – to your incredible team Michel. I love you dearly.

Message from the Old Man: *"Sometimes, one has to face his greatest fears to become a stronger individual. Running away is not always the solution. Breathe. Stay strong and surround yourself with bravery and trust. Difficult moments eventually dissipate. Always."*

ABOUT BEING INKED

The snow clouds have passed. The sun will shine today - and people's moods will lift. I know it. I sense it. Later on, today, some more ink to finish off this 'novel' theme. The journey of a story, then, now, on my forearm. You know, one day, if I am doomed to forget, I hope that these permanent drawings will take me back to simpler times, help me remember my many lives and propels me into so many memories ... I'll sit there, well into my 90's, smiling - reliving moments in my mind and soul - just because of the prompts I will still be receiving from looking at my shriveled arms. It's simple, and I find it's also very poetic. To each his own, hein?

Message from the Old Man: *"It's a brand-new day - yes - but did you ever consider that it could also be the beginning of a brand-new Life? Of a brand-new Adventure? We hold the power within ourselves to make changes and start Soul and Spirit revolutions - to make a difference - even a minuscule one - in the tapestry of the Universe. Yes - it's cold outside: but it's a great day to start!"*

ABOUT THE NEW YEAR

Life is always colored with happy moments - you simply have to be aware of them and make the best of every adventure, even if at times it seems like there is more angst or sadness associated with it.

Moreover, instead of deciding what my Spirit shall search for in 2019, I have chosen to go with the flow - and to let myself taste the different adventures which will come my way. I vow to give myself simple pleasures: good coffee, thick socks, new plants ... I plan on writing as much as I can and perhaps to finally be able to share the novel living within my heart and memories. I hope to be true to my Spirit's calling and to be able to help those around me - as best as I can. I hope to be strong for others when they lose their stamina, full of love and empathy when they forget to love themselves and a beacon of light when they feel that they've lost their way.

Along with my A-Team, I hope to connect more people with their inner desires and perhaps share messages of love when they doubt themselves. I hope to be Anne, just a slightly different version - version 2019. So that, my friends, makes me smile and thus, I look forward to whatever comes next.

ON PRESSING SEND

They say that when the teacher is ready, the student appears. (or is it the other way around?) As I grow older, this rings even stronger. The Universe seems to, as expected, have the perfect timing to every season in my Life. Whether it be because of personal circumstances, or in this case, professional ones, if one genuinely listens and pays attention, there are lessons to be grasped which apply to every aspect of our daily journeys. In this particular case, it happened in January. I am a high school teacher. The semester was ending, and we were getting ready to embark on a new one, which meant that I had to finalize details. I was likely one of the first ones to have her final reports completed. When the deadline came, and I missed it, Alain, my supervisor, nonchalantly showed up in my class one afternoon and started chatting with me. We talked about school events, music that we had recently discovered and about life in general. We often did this: he'd walk into my center, grab a chair, chat for a few minutes and then leave. We'd laugh and ponder events. He had the best jokes, and he felt genuinely comfortable amongst my students. He exuded respect for others, and it was reciprocal. His presence made my heart complete. He had (and still has) a way of finding a positive twist to things – and I cherished his frequent visits to my classroom. On that particular day, he looked at me and he 'felt' uncomfortable. Alain cleared his throat and asked: "Did you complete your report cards? You're the only one who hasn't submitted them yet ." I looked at him and nearly cried. I explained to him that I had completed them weeks ago, but that I couldn't bring myself to press 'send.' My mind was playing games with me: "Were they okay? Were they complete? Were they acceptable and fair"? Alain was stunned. I could tell from the little throbbing vein on his forehead that he never expected this from me. I, after all, looked strong and ready to tackle any challenge at any given time – yet I couldn't bring myself to press 'send.' That's when he looked at me, and in a very true-to-him voice, he offered to do it for me. I turned on my computer, logged into the program and seconds later, it was done. I was relieved, and he looked amused. I thanked him, and he just answered: "Next time, come and see me. We'll do it together".

The next few years held various other deadlines. When you have to answer to multiple Ministries and supervisors, reports are written and of course, sent off. There were other personal moments which saw me hesitate and almost lose incredible opportunities because I could not bring myself to share what I had written. I always doubted myself. It was never good enough, and through it, all, my dear friend Alain was- *and still is* - there. I texted him – and told him that I was 'looping,' and he'd answer: press SEND. It never got easier, but I knew that he was there, ready to help if I needed him to do so. That meant the world to me – and because of him, I made my way through other journeys. I heard his voice when I 'sent' off my doctoral thesis. It had been complete for weeks before I found the courage to do so.

I heard his voice when I submitted a song which I had composed. Again and again, Alain's voice resonated as I sent off my manuscript to my first book. It rang as I rekindled friendships with people, I had not seen in years by sending them messages. I wasn't about the task: it was about finding the courage to press 'send' – and to see what the Universe had planned when I did so. Were it not for him, my dearest friend Alain, I would have never experienced the satisfaction of true completion in many aspects of my Life, and for that, I am eternally grateful. *Je t'aime.*

Message from the Old Man: *"Find the courage within yourself to become whom you are truly meant to become. You are never alone. Through that of others around you, I send you the strength warranted to advance on your journey. Smile. Breathe and always press: send. Life is too short to live harvesting regrets of moments you didn't take."*

ABOUT ROYAL'S BOAT

Ten years ago, I made a massive change in my career. I had always been teaching in the same town, with the same individuals. Although I loved them dearly, events had happened that encouraged me to explore other avenues and I decided that it was time to move on. I eventually 'touched down' in high school where I teach now. There are roughly one thousand people that grace the hallways: young adolescents, colleagues, paraprofessionals – you get the picture. Amongst them is a person whom I admired so very much. His name is Royal. He is quiet. Intelligent. Witty. Funny. Talented. We became friends when he too would show up in my classroom, with chocolate bars, no less. We'd chat about life, remark on various current events and he'd be on his way, always happy and smiling. I loved how he graced my days with wit and energy. He personified integrity, and everybody loved his presence. One day, Royal came to me and was crying. He was diagnosed with cancer, and he didn't know where this adventure would leave him. "I don't want to die," he told me. "I have too much to live for – and this wasn't in my plans." I was stunned. I didn't know what to answer him, and so I sat with him in silence, and when he finished talking, he hugged me, and before he left, I told him that I would pray for him, every day until he got better. Months went by. My friend underwent numerous treatments which left him so very ill. He had headaches. He was cold and had no energy. His beautiful wife took care of him. She had started a social media page to keep us all updated and true to my word, I followed it diligently. Every day, as my day started, I sent out intents to perhaps make him smile and give him energy when the day would bring moments that were too difficult to bare. He came back to work – thinner and still sick. However, Royal was determined to prove to everybody – including himself – that Life was worth living – and that he wasn't done with this current journey. He came and went. Months passed, and my brave friend experienced many more ups and downs. He was hospitalized many times, and he fought with all of his might. Cancer does that to a person: it makes you stronger – then it destroys you and waits to see if you're going to make it back to your feet. Royal did just that and eventually went into remission. Last year, he sauntered into my class – and he was smiling. Life was not perfect – but he was feeling better and stronger. "Guess what?", he said. "I decided that Life was short and that I was meant to live it to the fullest. I downsized – and I bought myself a boat!" I smiled. Royal lives close to a beautiful lake in our city, and finally, he was going to get to enjoy rides as he wished. Although it was early in the season, it kept him going through the weeks that followed boating season. Whenever he'd feel down or wasn't feeling well, I'd remind him: "but you have a boat" …. And he'd smile. This year, as Spring approaches, I can't help but think of him. I still send him intentions every day. I know that there are days when he's feeling down and ill – but in the end – he always smiles. "I have a boat," he says. "And maybe, just maybe, I'll buy myself a snow machine too." This Summer, dear friend, you're taking me out on the lake. Xo

---

Message from the Old Man: *"In adversity and pain, remember that small things and special moments have the power to raise your energy and spirit. You are never alone. Enjoy Life with all of her moments: you were meant to enjoy all of them fully."*

ABOUT MY ARTIST

There are people in our lives that transcend time and distance. Though you may not remember the particular details of 'chance' encounters which lead you to become friends, it happens instantly, as though you have known them forever. Such is the case for one of my best friends, Leo, who also happens to be the incredible artist who gave life to the Old Man on the Bench's: bench. I'm smiling. We met in Grade 5 when his whole school moved to ours. Budgets were slashed, and the students became a permanent part of our student body. I guess Universe sort of 'forced' us to meet and to connect. It's just funny how growing up we all gravitate towards one another, just because we seem only to get along and share the same interests. As life advances, we notice that our journeys bring us on different paths. We often lose track of one another. Very often, we become strangers and merely choose to move on. Our friendship, however, was not like this. Years had passed, and we found ourselves teaching in the same school. Leo guided me during some of my most intense and difficult professional moments. He helped me see the pros and often cons of many of my impulsive decisions. I was never one to be calm, while the man seemed to exude it (and he, in fact – still does). As life advances, he is still very much a substantial part of a core circle of friendship and trust. I choose not to have large rings of people around me – yet he has always held a most magnificent space in my well-reserved heart. He is a kindred spirit. An artist. He is a dedicated worker and a man who has the utmost integrity. This soft-spoken man would give his life for the ones whom he loves and cherishes. I am forever grateful that his wife Joany, a beautiful, talented dancer, choreographer and writer allows me to share some of their precious time. It seems that everybody wants a piece of him – and because of her kindred understanding, I get to have an important one as well.

A few years ago, when I told him I'd be writing my first book, Leo immediately said to me that he'd draw my cover. I smiled. He is an internationally recognized artist – and to have him put his time and energy in my project meant the world to me. He became the person who gave life to the bench – that very same one that sits on the beach in North Bay to commemorate the incredible experience of a family friend. People have always loved and admired his work – but when he chose to offer the image of the bench to the world – I believe that the Universe smiled because Leo is, after all, quite a wise 'not-so-old' man. His presence is felt wherever he goes. He helps people. He soothes them. He shows them through example that Life is meant to live – and that you should make the best of every moment. He's also very handsome. "Chapeau mon ami. Thank you for being part of my current life journey. Thank you for being one of my cheerleaders, for helping so many around you – and simply for being: you". I couldn't have chosen a better friend with whom to sit on this bench of Life.

Message from the Old Man: *"Creativity takes courage. Sometimes, you will have to take some chances – Believe that you are never alone and that you are supported in your leap of Faith."*

FINAL THOUGHTS

It has been quite a journey since the Old Man made his first appearance in my life more than a year ago. A few days after officially launching the first volume of the series, my Father passed away, sending me into a tailspin of emotions and on the path which changed the course of my existence. Through careful observation and deep reflection, I have become even more aware of the presence of this incredible mystical force which unites us all. Often, because we become absorbed in the automation of our quotidian routines, we forget to stop and to listen to those around us. Life is filled with moments which have the mind-blowing power to alter the course of our passages, changing us, if we allow them to do so, for the better. The Old Man has continuously reminded me of this, sending me brilliant teachers in this classroom we so often take for granted: Life. I hope that through the shared conversations, you will be able to become more attentive to your own clues that He is also very present in your own days, just as I have had the privilege to do so.

May you continue to smile, to grow and to appreciate the incredible blessings present in your life. Love, love and love some more. Finally, may you let the Old Man embrace you always, on happy days and during darker times. You are never alone.

I'll see you on the bench …. xo.

AFTERWORD

History repeats itself. It has been more than a year since Leo and I sat at a café, discussing the final details of the first book. Since then, many of you have already found the bench, and have sent me a picture of yourself and friends sitting on it, pondering life. I hope that while you sat there, you felt the love and wisdom of the Old Man as you listened to His knowledge. If you haven't yet had the chance to make your way to the bench, Leo offers this new version of the map to help you locate it. Take your book. Grab a coffee and sit in silence. The Old Man will find you, I promise. And please, I have a request: when you see the bench, send me a picture of you sitting on it so that we are able to continue expanding the incredible circle of love surrounding us. As always, I am so excited to see you sitting there. And finally, Leo wants me to tell you that if your toes are wet, you've walked too far …
Funny guy xo

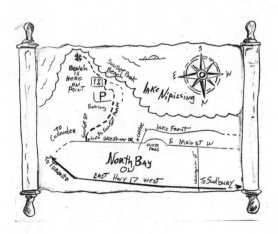

PEOPLE TO WHOM I OWE A GREAT DEAL OF GRATITUDE

- *To Bill, Alex, Marc-André and Elizabeth*: Thank you for continuing to support my crazy bigger than life ideas and for being my rock, while allowing me to soar within the realms of my imagination. You are my Life – and I will forever love you.

- *To my parents:* Thank you for encouraging me always to reach higher and to never give up on my dream of becoming a writer. I'm doing it and owe my love of reading and writing to you. You live within me and within my words. I love you.

- *To my brother:* Thank you for being my soundboard – over and over and over ... What an honor it is to have you as a brother. I love you.

- *To my incredible friends Chantal, Mélodie, Meagan, Nina, Denis, Pierre, Dominique, Alain, Cameron, Nathan, Ron, Michel, Eva, Royal, Sue, Joany, Leo and so many more:* How do you even 'handle' me and my ideas? Thanks for being part of my innermost personal circle and for allowing me to share my thoughts and some of your stories with people. I cherish you all.

- *To Linda, Stephanie and Lucien*: Thank you for allowing me to use your most beautiful bench as a source of inspiration to the World.

- **_To Yves:_** Thank you for reminding me that I must paint and write. I'll see you in the next book …

- **_To Leo:_** Thank you for being so patient with me and bringing my ideas to life. You keep me from getting lost in my thoughts … and in my directions. _Je t'aime._

- **_To Heather Plett_**: Thank you for teaching me _how to hold space_ for myself and for others. (read all about her work at _https://heatherplett.com_)

- **_To the many who inspire and enrich my life every day:_** Thank you for letting me share your moments and for being on my journey.

- **_To all the numerous unnamed individuals_** who continue to believe in my dream and keep reading what the Old Man has to share, I appreciate you from the bottom of my heart. Thank you for being there.

- **_And to you, Old Man:_** _What a year it's been! Thank you for allowing me to share your wisdom with so many across the World and for encouraging me to write this second book about our conversations. The journey is just beginning, as you often remind me while we sit on the bench. I'm ready! Thank you for being my anchor, my inspiration and my most significant source of inspiration. xo_

HOW TO REACH THE AUTHOR

Website:
https://annedaniellegingras.com

Facebook:
https://www.facebook.com/benchmoments/

Email:
oldmanonthebench4444@gmail.com

HOW TO REACH THE ARTIST

Facebook:
https://www.facebook.com/leo.levac.3

Instagram:
leolevac

Flickr:
levacart photo

Email:
leolevac@gmail.com

Printed in the United States
By Bookmasters